# [A] MYSTICAL KEY TO THE ENGLISH LANGUAGE

# [A] MYSTICAL KEY TO THE ENGLISH LANGUAGE

## Robert M. Hoffstein

Destiny Books
Rochester, Vermont

Destiny Books
One Park Street
Rochester, Vermont 05767

Library of Congress Cataloging-in-Publication Data

Hoffstein , Robert M.
    A mystical key to the English language / Robert M. Hoffstein
        p.    cm.
    Includes bibliographical references and index.
    ISBN 0-89281-309-1
    1. English language—Alphabet—Miscellanea. 2. Vocabulary—Miscellanea.
3. Occultism. I. Title.
BF 1623.A45H64 1992
133.3—dc20                                                    92-5615
                                                                  CIP

Printed and bound in the United States

10 9 8 7 6 5 4 3 2 1

Text design by Charlotte Tyler

Destiny Books is a division of Inner Traditions International, Ltd.

Distributed to the book trade in the United States by American International
Distribution Corporation (AIDC)

Distributed to the book trade in Canada by Book Center, Inc., Montreal, Quebec

To the memory of
Morris Frank,
Beloved friend,
Respected teacher.

# CONTENTS

PREFACE IX

INTRODUCTION 1

THE VOWELS 9

THE CONSONANTS 29

A SAMPLING OF SIMPLE COMBINATIONS 87

AN OVERVIEW 177

CONCLUSION 182

APPENDIX— EXAMPLES OF SOME
   EXTRAORDINARY WORDS 184

# PREFACE

How easily we take for granted the letters and sounds of the alphabet, those ABC's that both tickled and tormented us as children! For when we finally learned to shape meaningful words out of them ("'t-r-e-e-' makes 'tree'—Hooray!"), we somehow came to the conclusion that they themselves were only arbitrary symbols that lacked any meaning or interest in their own right. (If we chose, A could just as well be B, X could be Y, etc.) Indeed, when we grew older and had contact with other languages, this idea was powerfully reinforced. "Well," we reasoned, "we can call a tree 'tree' in English, *'arbre'* in French, and *'Baum'* in German, so what difference does it make what sound-combination we use, so long as it's practical and enables us to communicate successfully? No difference: The various languages must be so many *random* methods for arriving at the same end... Why, over there, for example, is the same leafy object, no matter how I refer to it! As Shakespeare observed:

> "What's in a name? that which we call a rose
> By any other name would smell as sweet."

A reasonable assumption, it seems. And yet, what if this long-established belief of ours were at best a half-truth? What if beneath the surface there was a treasure trove of meaning in the "arbitrary" characters that pour from our mouths, pens, and typewriters every day? In fact, what if the twenty-six building blocks of English (and letters of all languages) were keys to a great Wisdom-teaching that could "transform our lives if we but opened ourselves to it?"

The letter as "alive," as voice of the spirit—this, in a nutshell, is the fascinating claim of the present work, the inspiration that drives Robert M. Hoffstein to approach the English alphabet not merely as a device for "sculpting sound," but as an "enormously potent tool for self-reflection." With constant reference to mystic tradition and the Hebraic roots of our letters, the author attempts to show that (a) there is a native meaning in each letter of the alphabet, and (b) both the use of these letters and their alphabetical order tell a story, a primal myth regarding the transformation of Man. Even as DNA provides for our involuntary biological development, so this grand narrative answers to our voluntary, spiritual development; it inscribes in our soul a certain code, a basic structure, a Way of life that we ought to follow to the end. And what constitutes the Way? Briefly described, it is our God-given purpose of awakening from our everyday "Sleep," transcending our attachment to the things of the ego, and returning to our absolute Self.* It is the miracle of Enlightenment—

---

*It is important to note that Mr. Hoffstein's discoveries bear out in a significant manner the work of Maurice Merleau-Ponty, the French phenomenologist who is emerging as one of the most revolutionary thinkers of the twentieth century. According to Merleau-Ponty, the basic thrust of language is not to communicate neutral fact; it is, rather, to express the "emotional" or "gestural" sense of objects, for beneath factual data and our private subjective feelings, there is, on the deepest level, an active Essence at work in the world; and the "Logos" of this Being is that organizing power which stirs us to verbalize. Quite literally, our primal 'e-motions' are 'motions outward' toward articulating the "Self of the World" and rejoining it in word and deed. Thus, writing in 1945, Merleau-Ponty predicts that when the "emotional content" of language is someday analyzed, it shall be found that, despite appearances, no linguistic element is really arbitrary. On the contrary, ". . . words, vowels, and phonemes are so many ways of 'singing' the world and. . . their function is to represent things, not as the naive onomatopoeic theory had it, by reason of an objective resemblance, but because they extract, and literally express, their emotional essence." (Maurice Merleau-Ponty, *Phenomenology of Perception*, London: Routledge & Kegan Paul, 1962, p. 187.) And indeed, exactly thirty years after Merleau-Ponty's death, the author of the present volume has, in my view, confirmed this prediction. In every key from A to Z, the alphabet is a magnificent Song of Creation; and our sacred task is to vocalize it with all our heart, and with all our soul, and with all our might.

that ideal of the "perennial philosophy" which haunts our collective unconscious across all cultures and eras. For as Jung, Campbell, and numerous other
investigators have made clear, we yearn to drink of the Holy Grail, despite
every effort to repress our thirst in the name of a superficial realism. It is the
"impossible dream" dreamt by the "impossible" Quixote in each of us; and if
ignorant fools are forever telling him to abandon the quest, nevertheless this
wisest of fools will insist on raising his lance and penetrating our common-
place rites and symbols—including the very marks of our speech: Or how else
explain the universal theme of death and rebirth which pervades not only the
Grail of Christianity but every sacrament of the major religions? Deny this
central injunction, convince us that we do not have to lose our life in order to
save it, and the banished truth will inevitably reappear on the margins of our
awareness, (as in such subtly influential "occult" movements as Qabbalism,
alchemy, Swedenborgiansim, theosophy, etc.)

From sleep to Illumination, from ego-enslavement to liberation—this is
the path which Mr. Hoffstein finds laid out in the very units of our writing.
Like magic runes, the ABC's that we acquired so many years ago spell out
nothing less than the most important message of our lives! And to take that
message to heart is be perfectly—spellbound.

Ernest Sherman
Associate Professor of Philosophy
Pace University, Pleasantville, N.Y.
February 1991

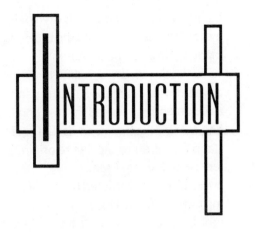

# INTRODUCTION

What started me on this alphabetical odyssey was an intriguing thought I had in my early twenties, that somehow, if I knew the sound of, say an apple—not the usual sound we ascribe to it, but the secret, qabbalistic sound—then I would be able to materialize it by merely invoking this inner sound. The idea gripped me in a strange, mystical way. I sensed that it just had to be so.

Morris Frank, my true friend and respected teacher, familiarized me with the esoteric Hebrew alphabet. For him it mirrored an ancient teaching, one that was in harmony with the Old and New Testaments. He spoke eloquently of the Aleph-Beth, seeing the letters as signs for metaphysical concepts that summarized the history of "inner world"—a world common to all mankind.

I'll never forget my excitement when I heard him say that the last four letters of the Hebrew alphabet (Koph, Resh, Shin, Tau) spelled out KRST—CHRIST! I was only twenty-two at the time and with my youthful enthusiasm thought I would try it out on a *yeshiva bucher* friend of mine. For him, the Talmud was the only orthodox study; Qabbalah was out of bounds—"evil." I laughingly told him, point blank, that Christ was hidden in his own alphabet in a way that he would never suspect. He looked at me with wide open eyes, anxious to hear what I was about to say, ready to pounce on me for my unorthodox leanings. I simply repeated that "Christ" was the

1

grand finale, the coda of his own beloved Aleph-Beth. Instead of berating me, as I thought he would, he broke out into a sweat. The "revelation" had made quite an impact on him!

I never devoted much time to Gematria. Amazing relations can be discovered with it, I'm sure,* but my soul yearned for something more essential. Somehow, I sensed that the English alphabet (along with the Hebrew, and many others) was in itself a secret teaching, and if we could understand the letters as they were originally meant to be understood, the mystery would reveal itself.

Morris Frank restricted his meditations to the Hebrew alphabet. Following through to the English was the logical next step. Surely there were etymological connections. Most of the world's alphabets are believed traceable to an unknown Mother Alphabet, for there are too many similarities to rule out the possibility of a common origin.

What I have unearthed is hopefully more than just a "dead carcass."† It is the traces of a remarkable mystery teaching buried in the midst of our own English alphabet, a teaching that may well transform our lives if we can open ourselves to it.

Probably the most serious criticism that can be leveled against my efforts is the failure to stick to orthodox etymologies, favoring instead esoteric ones. For example, the word *skull* is etymologically related to *shell* as the word *scholar* is to *school*. I have no quarrel with this. The skull is a bony case, and as such it is a kind of shell; and a scholar belongs to a school. Officially, skull and scholar have no etymological connection, but it is clear that they have an esoteric one. For who hasn't seen old paintings of a scholar, deeply engrossed in thought, with the proverbial skull on his desk? Symbolically, the skull reminds the scholar of his mortality, forcing him

---

*For example, the numerical equivalent of the Hebrew word for "gods"— *elohim*—placed around the circumference of a circle reads, in sequence, 31415 (the ratio *pi*). This strange "coincidence" implies that the ancient Hebrews understood the relationship between the center (actually the diameter) of a circle and its circumference, and were describing on another level the relationship between spirit and matter, or the extent of God's Kingdom.
†In the wonderful Arabian Nights story "The Fisherman and the Jinni," the first three castings brought up a dead ass, a broken pot, and some shards. Only on the fourth try did the fisherman pull in his life-threatening liberation, a bottled up jinni.

to rethink his position on life per se, the wellspring of all scholarship. Thus there is an inner relationship between *skull* and *scholar* that is lost if one does not look beneath the surface. The scholar, in contemplating the skull, realizes that in order to be a scholar in the true sense of the word (skull-or) he must die to himself as Christ did. That kind of knowledge is bestowed only upon a "dead" man—a skull.

Ancient mystery schools probably taught these concepts, but today orthodox etymologists affix the label "folk etymology" to these types of relationships, passing over them as unworthy of their thought, or perhaps "interesting," in the same way that old wives' tales are "interesting." But to dismiss the inner relationship between skull and scholar is to throw away an important key that could open many doors. Humankind is time bound, locked into historical time, but we also transcend time. So does language.

Other examples will help make my point clear. The word *lesson* is related to the Middle English *lessoun* and to the Latin *lectro*—a reading. This is all well and good, but it fails to make a statement about the simple construction of the word itself which is important if one wishes to gain a better idea of the concept that conceived the word in the first place. Esoterically, *lesson* can be read as *less on*. Now, the ordinary Eastern understanding of a lesson is to "add on" to one's store of knowledge. In school the usual lesson adds more information to what we already know. A scholar becomes a virtual encyclopedia of facts. But the esoteric understanding, written right into the word itself, is that the "lesson" for the soul is to "unlearn" or strip away, and bare the essence, in a search for the "thing-in-itself" that animates all life.*

---

*If there is no "apperceptive mass" or receptivity, for this sort of teaching, no amount of explaining will convince someone that this approach to the meaning of words is useful. Indeed, it could be labeled "arbitrary" and dismissed as irrelevant or a curiosity. It is important to point out here that this approach is, in essence, anything but arbitrary.

A critic may concede that it is of anagrammatic interest to break up the word into "less on," but he will maintain that this is just arbitrary playfulness and has no legitimate place in serious scholarly research. In support of this contention he could argue that it is just as valid to break up the word into les-son, less-son or less-sun, which alters the meaning entirely and throws my interpretation of "less-on" into a cocked hat. But does it? For surely, if a man is a man (or a lesson

It can be argued that etymologists are in a different business, and their main interest is in tracing a word's *historical* roots, which is a legitimate pursuit. It is, but there is no reason to stop there. It is interesting to note, for example, that the word *clew (clue)* derives from a root word meaning *ball* or *skein,* which symbolically relates to Ariadne's ball of thread in the Labyrinth. Why the letters that go to make up *clew* mean *ball* or *skein* is never addressed. What I'm saying is that when a word is traced back to its source, the root word that launched it will in all probability, shed very little light on the essential meaning of the word itself.

Take, for example, the word Mass. Historically, it can be traced to the Latin phrase, *"Ite, missa est"* (Go, you are dismissed"). In time, *missa* became *masse* and later *mass.* But this ignores the inner meaning completely which is important if we are to begin to understand what Christian Mass is all about—how it relates to us and to the evolution of our souls. To stop with *"Ite, missa est"* is to settle for the husk instead of the kernel.

---

is a lesson) he is a man no matter how you split him, in all aspects and from all dimensions. Cut him up, run him through a wringer, analyze his blood—he is still a man, though different facets of the man will be revealed. Likewise with *lesson,* or any other word understood in its "naked splendor." If one does not intuit the meaning it is lost. This can be said of any art or science. The bottom line is that to appreciate these subtle variations on a meaning there must be something of the poet in the person.

In this spirit the word "lesson," when broken up into its components will, like the monad, reflect the life within it.

*Less-sun* can be understood to mean less light. The grand lesson for Man is to descend into matter where he experiences the "dark night of the soul." The story of Abraham also depicts the loss of this light when he is commanded by God to sacrifice his "son" (*less son*). That is to say, can Abraham survive without his most precious possession—less (his) son?

*Lesson* can also be divided phonetically into *le-son* or *le-sun.* Lesson here is likened to the light of the sun. (The *le* is the definite article *the.*) It is that Light which consumes all the dross: less-on.

Reversed, lesson reads *nossel,* which can be rendered either *nozzle* (the S and Z are closely related) or *nos-el* the "nose" of El or God. Thus, a lesson from this perspective is to savor and to appreciate the essence of a thing; the nose knows!

By and large then, by contemplating each letter of *lesson* one may reconstruct the quintessential elements of the mystery teaching behind the word.

It is true that merely to point out that the word *lesson* is a contraction of *less on*

There is no etymological relationship between the words *devil* and *develop,* but there is an esoteric one. Why do they sound so much alike? Likewise with *damn* and *dam*—they are related, but not etymologically. Once an inner relationship is established, why those *specific* letters? For example, what meaningful relationships can be found among the words, *mom, mum,* and *mime,* and why the M to begin with?*

Who would think that an ox (the hieroglyphic meaning of the Hebrew Aleph from which the English letter A derives) has anything to do with the prefix A meaning *not* or *without* (as in *asexual* or *aseptic*)? But there is an esoteric relationship, and it goes much further. What is the essence of an ox? Why was an ox chosen to represent the Aleph in the first place, and what does it mean to the inner self? What relationship does the letter A have to the B, the C, and the D? Does the alphabet tell a coherent story?

Another argument that can be advanced is that what has been unearthed may apply to English but certainly not to French, Spanish, or other languages. The word *man,* for instance, may lend itself to alphabetic analysis

---

is limiting. It points to only one aspect of the word. *But it is not arbitrary.* For, if the essence is grasped, seen from any angle it reflects the light of the word's primordial meaning.

This is subject to error, of course. That is where arbitrariness enters the picture, for the poet who attempts to bring down the sacred fire could be flawed. There are errors in my interpretations because I am not a perfect vehicle. Only a Christ, a Buddha, or a being of that nature could measure up fully to this task. What I hope is that at least a "dim light" shines through and that my inspiration has caught some semblance of eternal truth.

Nor does every combination in the English language (or for that matter in any language) spell out a meaningful message. *Come, coma,* and *comma* can be reduced to a common denominator implying stoppage, but not all CM-MC words follow this pattern. There is no perfect fit. It is not airtight. However, although points do fall outside of the line, there is still a pattern to be discovered. An order emerges, hidden to the casual eye, that underlies the babel of tongues. Call it an "implicate order" (Bohm) if you will, the still small voice of the soul of language is whispering to Man.

Mull over the contents of this book, and if it's not "perfect" to your way of thinking, bring your own light to it. I hope that it will shine more brightly for you. *Actually, the etymological rendering and the esoteric rendering should complement each other, as different levels of expression. But corruptions and distortions of one sort or another usually rule out the possibility.

in English, but what about *homme* in French or *hombre* in Spanish?

The word *flower* is generic; it includes roses, daisies, buttercups, lilacs and many others. So is the word *man*. In English a single aspect may be emphasized, in French another, and so on. The H and O of *homme* can be seen as added elements that reveal the concept of "man" in a slightly different light.* Actually, the alphabet itself is kaleidoscopic. Turn it a bit and the letters reposition themselves, creating new patterns. In the last analysis the alphabet serves not only as a means for sculpting sound but also as an enormously potent tool for self-reflection.

It is easy to forget that the reader himself has to "animate" language, that the esoteric "meaning" is not inherent in the words. Take, for example, the word *God*. *What does it mean?* Ten thousand things to ten thousand different people, with overlaps, but enough serious differences to cause concern. To some God is made out of whole cloth, a mere product of fancy. To others he/she/it is an entity "out there" with an independent existence. There are countless other views in between. The words *liberty, life, justice, freedom, good, evil, right, wrong, morality, ethics*—even the word man—are subject to many interpretations. No matter how carefully one defines these words given the circumstances of our present mode of understanding, other meanings can be read into them. That is why we find it so difficult to communicate with our fellows, and even with ourselves. For no sooner do we say one thing than we think another. War to some is peace to others. This is not an accident of the language; it is built into the very nature of humanity. Language only echoes the contradiction. (Rudolph Steiner defined man as "a contradiction come to life.") The curse of contradiction could be transformed into a blessing† if only we could see it. But alas, as Gurdjieff so wisely said, we are "third force blind"; we do not see the Holy Ghost. Without the balance of the third eye of the Spirit, we will forever destroy ourselves, the yeas lining up against the nays, the Communists against the Capitalists, the Arabs against the Jews, and so on. It is written into the word *life* itself. Reversed it reads *efil* (evil). In other words, life

---

*This is also true of alphabets other than those related to Latin. On the surface, this may not seem to be the case, but an underlying pulse is common to them all.
†And this blessing is that every word seeks its opposite to complete itself, to be whole again; for fundamentally there is only One Word and all (lower case) words are fragments of That!

can either be "good"—life per se—or "evil" depending on how one lives it. But even this is subject to many interpretations, as some will surely argue that life *is* evil—backwards *and* forwards!

All of language, then, should be read with the Inner Eye. Otherwise, it is impossible to understand anything. When we read, we add an essential ingredient to the word, an ingredient that transforms it to our own level of understanding. To the extent that this transformation is on the level of a Christ, a Moses, or a Buddha we can understand the word impartially. To the extent that we fail to reach these heights our understanding will suffer, and, as a consequence, our "world."

The reader will learn as the book unfolds that the "message" of the English alphabet concerns itself with inner evolution, our "descent into matter" and our return to the source. In short, it is a treatise on the transformation of Man. Indeed, MAN is the fulcrum of the alphabet. This can be illustrated in a striking way, for counting from A, the thirteenth letter is M, and counting back from Z, the thirteenth letter is N. Thus, MN are the two "middle" letters of the alphabet. Animate them with the A (the First Principle—the Breath of Life) and *Man* is hidden in the midst of his own creation, and as such has a responsibility for balancing it.

The word *alphabet* itself owes its origin to the first two letters of the Greek alphabet—*Alpha* and *Beta* (*Aleph, Beth* in Hebrew). Hidden in this construction is a third letter that has been overlooked: the Hebrew letter *Pe*, meaning mouth, and so by extension the speech of Man. Thus, the word alphabet can be rendered *al-pe-bet*, with *Al*, the first syllable, meaning God (Al—Allah); *Pe*, the second, indicating speech; and *Bet*, the third, meaning house. Thus the alphabet is the sound of God voiced through the Temple (house) of Man, the sound "vehicle" who amplifies the sound of God. Contemplate the alphabet and wonder about the grandeur of its construction, and you will discover how close this definition comes toward catching a glimpse of its real splendor.*

In this book I attempt to reconstruct the metaphysical bones of our English alphabet. Every word (if it is not too thoroughly corrupted) can be

---

*The sounds of the letters themselves and how they relate to meaning are barely touched on in this book, and will have to wait for another chapter in the history of our attempts to understand the Logos. I suspect, however that to know the Sound is to be able to create the world!

traced back to a metaphysical infrastructure. Once the "man" is remembered, everything else can be derived. The word "kill," for example, in one of its primal senses means "compression of the light." Thus when we read in the Old Testament that Cain *kills* his brother Abel, we can begin to contemplate what it could mean.

In the last analysis, words are in no way arbitrary sounds. When used with reverence, they reflect the Presence of the Logos that *is* our Life.

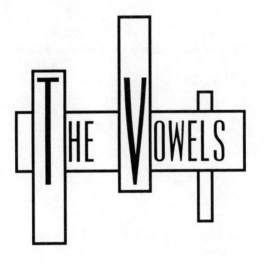

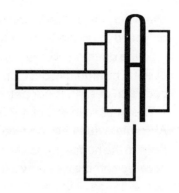

The letter A, as keynote, sets the tone for the entire alphabet. It is derived from the Semitic Aleph (meaning ox). The ox is a castrated bull. Its seed has been sacrificed for the sake of a greater work, that of helping the farmer plant the seed that will nourish mankind.

For all practical purposes it is not wise to harness a bull to a plow, for periodically its enormous energies are directed toward reproducing its kind. The ox, however, has given up its seed and can concentrate its energies on the planting and harvesting of grain. It is not distracted by a drive to reproduce. The essence is simple and can be summed up in one word: Sacrifice. Something must be given up for the purpose of receiving something else. If a vessel is not first emptied, it cannot be filled.

The word *sacrifice* means *to make sacred* or, in a broader sense, *to make whole;* the lesser is sacrificed for the greater. The sacrifice of the ox's seed is, of course, symbolic. True sacrifice is the sacrifice a great soul must undertake (on the level of Christ, Moses, or Buddha) to help sustain the world. For without that kind of sacrifice the world would die of spiritual malnutrition. This principle of sacrifice (or giving up of one's seed) is so much a part of the letter A that even in its present form it has retained its hieroglyphic

11

character. Invert the A, and one can readily see a crude hieroglyph of an ox yoked to do the work of Man ($\forall$).*

So the opening note is struck, and it is based on sacrifice, the giving up of self. The alphabet develops this theme; indeed it can be seen as a secret code that describes our potential for spiritual development.

The letter A, in one of its connotations, stands for the First Principle, the Absolute, which has no face, form, or figure and is totally incomprehensible to the human mind. As such it is often designated as a negative quality because nothing we know can describe it. Thus, A, often means *not* or *without,* as in asexual, anesthesia, asymptote, agnostic, achromatic, aseptic, and so on.

This attribute of negation, descriptive of the First Principle, is echoed in the symbol of the ox or castrated bull, whose seed is negated and given up for the sake of the harvest.

The A as prefix can also mean *separated, departed from, turned away,* or *broken off*—a shade removed from the A's archetypal negation. Consider, for example, avert, abrupt, abhorrent, abscond, absent etc.

A as suffix often converts a masculine name into a feminine one, as in

---

*An ox can be seen as a symbol for squaring (X) the circle (O); for the cross is the world of "four corners" (the square), while the circle is the Spirit (with no beginning and no end). To square the circle is to equate Spirit and matter, which *mathematically* is impossible. (In other words, the area of the polygon inside the circle can never precisely be equated to the area of the circle, although it comes tantalizingly close!) But "spiritually" it is required of us! Now it seems as though it can never be done, for the logicians among us, the mathematicians, have proved it to be impossible. To their way of thinking, contradiction is next to anathema. It destroys their system. But for the Spirit, contradiction is the substratum of life, its *sine qua non.*

How does one go about squaring the circle, then? The ox is one clue to the mystery, for it has given up its seed and therefore its "life". It has made a sacrifice worthy of the name of man, who is called upon to solve the equation of his existence, which is none other than X=O, or OX. Understood in this light, the OX becomes the crux ansata, the sacred symbol of life. It also can be seen as the male (X or angular) and the female (O or curvilinear) or the sacrifice of Oneness for the sake of the Child—the Son of Man.

The pentagram, pentacle, or "pentalpha" (five alphas or Alephs) with its projecting "A" at each corner is related to the "horns" of the ox. This fiery star of

Robert to Roberta, Theodore to Theodora, Frederick to Frederica, Carl to Carla, and Henry to Henrietta. The male is yang, or active, the female is yin, or receptive, because she is the receiver of the seed. The letter A, therefore, is also a feminine identifier because as First Principle she is the womb or ground out of which all life emerges.

As indefinite article, the A is placed before a noun to share with it the dignity of the Absolute. We read *a* book, see *a* sight, love *a* woman, enjoy *an* apple, as if to say that no object—no thing—is separate from the Absolute, or First Principle. The ocean is in the drop, or the "A" is in the Man. It is still "indefinite" and unformed, reflecting the Absolute's formlessness.

These derivative meanings of A can all be traced back to the A as First Principle. Consider, for instance, A as *one*, as in *a tree*, indicating *one* tree. Surely it is easy to see the connection, for the A, as Absolute, the All or One. Thus the One, paradoxically, has come to mean *All* (as in *All is One*), and less than All (*one* as subdivision).

As our study of the alphabet proceeds it will become apparent that contrary to Aristotelian thought, the letters, and words themselves, can become their own opposites. Not only does A mean *without, away,* or *separated from,* it can also mean *to* or *moving toward,* as in *ascend, achieve, admit, adore, assert,* etc. Thus the A completes a cycle of moving away from its center by returning and moving toward, to, or together with it again. This kind of polarity is built into our language. Each letter, therefore, has at least "two ends."

---

the ancients, symbol of Man and his nature (1—Spirit + 4—Matter = 5—Man, the "quint-essence") is nothing more than a five-fold letter A. In other words, the concept of Man ("5") can be equated with the concept of Sacrifice (the A). Man, therefore, is the end result (or fruit) of that sacrifice of the Sun (the pentagram or star) which is none other than the Son (Christ) of God! As "pentalpha," Man is the Extinguished Sun (the dead or sacrificed star) ever seeking to rediscover (rekindle) his Lost Light.

In this connection, the five wounds of Christ, four to his extremities (matter) and one to his side (actually "inside" the quintessence!), highlight the sacrifice (the piercing power of the arrow-shaped A that Christ exemplifies.

The fruit most often associated with the Fall of Man is the apple; for to cut one open (at right angles to the stem and through the middle) is to discover a pentacle, or five A's radiating out from the center. It is Man seen as "fallen star"—the bull that became an ox, or the Great Sacrifice of the Lord Absolute for the sake of His creation.

There are gradations in between, and A as prefix can also mean, *in contact with,* or *on,* as in *afire* and *ashore.* Here the A has more than "moved toward" and is "together again." Actually, the A, as Absolute, is in touch with all things.

The letters are dynamic forces, never quite standing still. Even the ineffable A (ineffable because as First Principle it cannot be truly comprehended) separates from itself—the Primal Sacrifice—and then returns to complete the cycle.

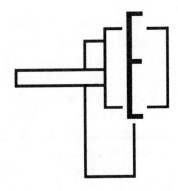

Historically, the E* is related to the Semitic *Heh* (or *window*), symbol of Universal Life. Just as the window lets in light, so does the light of the A stream through the window (lens) of the mind. Likewise, the primal A constricts (narrows down), to become the breath of man—his life.

This transformation of A to E is the first step in the individuation process essential to spiritual development.

This initial retraction (cf. the Qabbalistic concept of Tsimtsum or limitation) of the A as reflected in the E is actually inscribed in the meaning of the letter itself. Broadly speaking, the E is constrictive, whereas the A (echoing the Absolute) is expansive. The most general meaning of E as prefix is *out of,* as in *extra*-corporeal (outside of the body), *emit, eject, egress, exit, emanate, effusive, ecstasy* (to stand outside of the self), or *exist*. The sun rises *out of* the *East,* pointing to the E—as the concentrated light of the sun—arising out of the Primal A. The A, in this respect, is *istence,* the E, *existence* (or the light emerging from the Absolute A). And so, the word *be*—to exist.

*Ea* is the Babylonian god of the waters; that is, he emerges *out of* the depths (the Void, or A). A terrified person screams "EEEEEEEEE!", a sound

---

*The form of the E is considered by some scholars to represent a stick figure of a human being raising its arms (⊔⊔) in the act of rejoicing or celebrating life.

descriptive of the concentrated, constricted intensity of an emotional re-action to stress. (Cf. the expansive, ecstatic "ahhhh!") This natural sound has been incorporated into the word eerie—the impact or thrust of life in a confined space, the space of E or the space of emergent light.

Consider the word see* as it relates to vision, which is possible only through the lens of the mind. A lens limits the field, narrows down, con-centrates and focuses the light. (Cf. seed—the concentrated essence or "vision" of the plant.)

The sound of E is restrictive; (it reduces the Primal Light of A), so it also serves as diminutive. Consider, for example, the sound of words mommy, daddy, doggy, baby, dolly, and Bobby. Words that fall into this category usually imply affection because a reduction in size generally evokes a ten-der, nurturing response, it brings out our love. Without this love, the Great Experiment of Nature— becoming as "Nothing," or the transformation of the Infinite A to the Finite E— could not succeed. For God to give up (or sacrifice) his only Son, there must be in our nature a love that surpasses understanding.

Within the context of the sound of A as generally expansive, and the sound of E as generally constrictive, consider the following examples: Hell is known for its confinement, while a hall (like the great hall of a castle) is generally more expansive. A well usually brings to mind a narrow aper-ture out of which water is drawn; a wall generally encloses a larger space. An ell measures about forty-five inches, while all includes everything. Tall tends to be expansive, while tell is to relate, reckon with, enumerate, count the individual incidents, as in a story. Pale lacks intensity, while peal is the intense sound of a bell. To pray, ideally, is more expansive (reaching out to a Supreme Being), while to prey is to pillage, plunder, pounce upon. Lake presents a larger version of leak. Wake is more expansive than weak, The concept of man is all-inclusive, while men refer to individuals within this category. Make surely is more expansive than meek. There are more possibilities in may as opposed to me, which is more confining, restricted to self. To sail is to be open to the wind, to move vigorously, but to seal is to shut off. A fable is a related sequence of events, while feeble tends to

---

*The homonym sea, as the ancient mirror of the sun (upon which it can see its own reflection), is esoterically (not etymologically) related.

fall apart. *Fate* paints a broader picture, while a *feat* refers generally to a specific act. *Plate* is flat, open, while *pleat* is folded over. To *play* is to move lightly, a *plea* is more directed, targeted. *Mass* tends to move toward larger quantities, while *mess* usually refers to a portion, as in a *mess* of porridge.

*Back* tends to be broader than *beak*. *Main* generally applies to more open (as in a broad expanse), while *mean* "closes in". To *eat* refers to the narrowed spectrum of "now"—*an emerging point*—while *ate* projects the activity to the broader spectrum of the past. There are exceptions to this "rule" of sound, for A and E can generate their own opposites, a phenomenon that characterizes language in general. Meanings can also overlap, as in *meet* and *mate*. But there is a tendency for the A to be broad and the E narrow, echoing the archetypal, infinite A and the finite, emerging E.*

---

*The E, acting along lines of its ancient heritage, is the "silent activator" in many words changing the softer, broader sound (the undifferentiated First Principle) into a more intense, concentrated one (individuation). Consider the following examples: *rat* to *rate*, *bit* to *bite*, *hat* to *hate*, *sit* to *site*, *mit* to *mite* etc. It echoes the coalescence of life from a formless energy field to endless worlds or countless forms. The E focuses the light of A.

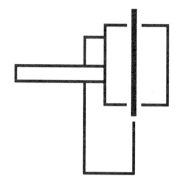

The third vowel, I, owes its origin to the Semitic *Yod,* or *hand:* that which grasps. The I is the "hand" of the mind, seeking to grasp the nature of truth as related to self (the individual I) and the world inhabited by the individual self.

The I stands midway between the five major vowels; it also stands midway between the man and his word. What is on one side is considered *self;* what is on the other, *not-self.* The I intermediates. It serves as a fulcrum or balance.

Thus it serves as a *connective* in such words as *dentiform, triform, semicircle, hemisphere, clavichord, omnivorous,* and *aurifer.* In words like *Israeli, Iraqi,* and *Punjabi* it means *of,* or *connected to.**

The I can also generate plurals (*alumni, radii, banditti*), for the I stands between the self and the world and partakes of both the singular and the plural. The self (or I) is legion.

Since the I is the organ of self as well as the organ of sight (eye), it is related to E, the emergent light. In the noun *Israeli,* as in so many other words,

---

*Very few "pure" English words terminate in I. (Punjabi is a "foreign" word.) Y or IE is used instead. Perhaps the unconscious reason for this is that the I (ego) should never follow or be "last" but appear only "up front," at the beginning. In other cultures the I serves—it follows.

the I assumes the sound of E. They are often coupled together, as in the name *Goldstein,* and are likely to be pronounced either as I or as an E.

The modern lower-case i has a dot over it, which reminds one that over each individual "I" (or ego) there is yet another "eye" (bindu), symbolizing the "eye over the eye." That "still small light" is the ego's true source of illumination. It adorns only the lower-case (or fallen I), for when the Greater Light is contacted (the upper-case I), the higher and lower light merge and the eye becomes single.*

The I is the smallest letter of the alphabet, as is the Yod in Hebrew. Like the mustard seed, it has enormous potential for growth, but also the inner strength to remain "a still small voice"—to be humble. The smallness of the I also reflects the constriction of the Spirit (the concept of Tsimtsum) in manifestation.

---

*Incidentally, the eye, as organ of the sun, can be likened to a microcosmic reproduction of it: compare the lashes to the rays, the elliptical shape to the orbiting earth, and the eyeball itself to the sun (☼). As above, so below.

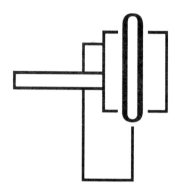

Scholars disagree over the origin of the letter O. Some derive it from the Semitic *Vau,* or nail; others from *Ayin,* or eye. It is often difficult to pinpoint origins. The origin of the alphabet itself is lost in history.

Our foremost concern here is the *sense* of the letter—the impact it makes on the soul. The letter O is in the form of a cipher—a zero, or nothing. Curiously, in the sequence of vowels it follows the I, which can also stand for the numeral one (1). Thus the I and the O can be read together as ten (10), the number of completion. One (1) is manifestation, existence, the emergence of life; zero (0) is istence, or non-existence (the state of the A in potential, before manifestation).

Perhaps the difficulty of assigning a secure origin to O lies in its inherent meaning—*nothing!* For indeed, where do we place something that is not! How can we affix it to any *thing?* That O is often traced back to the *Ayin* or eye suggests that "objective seeing," seeing a thing as it is without prejudice, depends on "emptiness." If the self of the observer is reduced to nothing, then and only then can seeing be truly objective and non-judgmental. The seer becomes the perfect mirror of the seen. That the letter O is also connected to the Semitic *Vau,* meaning to join (its hieroglyphic rendering is a *nail* or a *hook*), is more than just coincidental; the Zero Presence, which the O symbolizes, is a Presence (like the A or *Aleph*) connected to all things, without which connection all of manifested life would collapse. It is the *wu wei* of the East or the *thohou wa-bohou** of the Old Testament. Indeed, like the I, the O is also used a a connective in such words as *dorsocaudal, retroflex, socioeconomic,* and *psychosexual.*

As an interjection the O is used to express the surprise, fear, or wonder the Zero Presence inspires in us. For how can it be that all manifested life—existence—issues forth from No thing—that which is not? The letter O is the King of all koans.

One of the mysteries of O as circle is that it is circumscribed. That is to say, "Nothing" is made manifest by limitation, by enclosure in a sphere or a world. This is the paradox of paradoxes: in order to be seen, the Zero Presence condenses or constricts itself, and by an act of limitation (Tsimtsum in the Qabbalah) becomes visible as a pinpoint of light or a Zero (0). The O elegantly symbolizes this, for as "zero" it is nothing, yet having collapsed onto itself it became a world. All the stars we see, our own sun and moon, are the Zero Presence revealed.

O, when prefixed to some Irish surnames (O'Brien, O'Hara) refers to descendant, for the O (like the A) represents the source of our being. *Ob* is an obsolete word for sorcerer, a man who manipulates the forces of life (B)[†] and death (or O). (Cf. the Latin *obit,* death.) *Ob* as prefix has several shades of meaning, but generally speaking the sense is *to* or *toward, over, against (obey, observe, oblique, obrogate, obscure); completely, thoroughly (obdurate, oblivion, obfuscate); inverse order (obconic, obcordate, obovate); incompletely (obrotund, obround).* The all-inclusive presence of O accounts for *to, toward, over, against, completely,* and *thoroughly.*

The O plays a vital part in the words *ovum* and *oogenesis* because the egg, like the O, encircles new life. In the sacred word *OM,* the Zero Presence is immersed in manifestation (M).[‡]

---

*Without form and void (Gen. I:2), or as d'Olivet translates it: "contingent-potentiality in a potentiality-of-being. . . " (Fabre d'Olivet, *The Hebraic Tongue Restored,* p. 29 of *The Cosmogony of Moses.* New York and London: G. P. Putnam's Sons, 1921, translated by N. L. Redfield).

[†]Refer to the meaning of "B" under that heading.

[‡]See also the word *OM* in the Consonant section under M.

Consider the word *owe* and how its meaning is related esoterically to the letter O: The debt we "owe" (0) for the gift of life bestowed upon us by the Zero Presence is nothing less than our lives (our selves). What must be sacrificed, what we "owe" to our Creator, is the self that is illusory, or "nothing" (0). To understand this paradox is to possess* the world's greatest treasure.

---

*Etymologically "owe" is related to "own"— to have or possess. Thus, what you owe, you owe to your Self. Man has been cut off from his own Treasure. Like Jack and the Beanstalk, he is the rightful owner but has long since forgotten. To realize this is "to pour the empty (O) into the empty" (O).

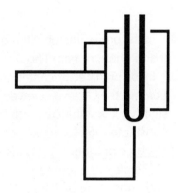

Historically, the U is related to the Semitic *Vau* (meaning *nail*). As vowel it is the fifth circle of light and can be paired with the third vowel, I, to become "Thou." Actually, the name of the letter U indicates its function in the sequence of vowels. It is the "you" in the I-Thou relationship. More simply put, it is the Not-I, or *other*.

In the U the cleavage or duality is complete. Now there can be man *and* wife, Cain and Abel, and all the other pairs of opposites. Man finds himself in the world and has to learn how to relate to an other, the not-I, or U. The construction of the letter U presents the story pictorially. Standing upright, side by side, are two "I's" that are seemingly separate but are joined by underground roots; the I and Thou are one.

The letter U coupled with the letter N (q.v.) generates the prefix *un,* meaning *not* (as in *unhappy, unfed, unwed*). It reflects the "you" projected outward (Adam's wife—in Latin, his *uxor** or opposite).

---

**Uxor* (Latin for wife—cf. *uxorial*) is a marvelously expressive word, that can be defined (by alphabetic analysis) as the will of man (R, q. v.) emerging from the unknown depths (X, q. v.). The vowels U and O thus breathe life into these consonants, reinforcing their meanings (U as "Adam's wife: that which opposes, and is also connected with him; and O as the Presence that identifies them as one Being).

In the prefix *uni* (one) the *un* (not-I) conjoined with the I generates unity (I and Thou, or I *am* Thou).

In the prefix *eu* (meaning *well, good, or true,* as in *eugenis, eudaemonia, eulogy*), the U can be viewed as essentially harmonious, pleasing, or good, signifying that this step into the world, this movement outward (creation), constitutes life. One must be "opposed" in order to create. Although U is a source of friction,* it is also a source of warmth and love.

The affixed e (eu) serves as ballast for the extended U, lighting its way and impressing on it that it is still connected to the Source of Light, which is pleasing to its "ears"—*eu-phony!*

---

*Recall that the U owes its origin to the *Vau* (nail), or that which joins. In the joining of the I and Thou for the ultimate realization that I *am* Thou, much friction has to be overcome, but it is friction that creates the heat necessary for fusion!

# SUMMARY

The initial A, out of which all the other vowels arise, represents the formless ground (the *Ungrund* of Boehme). Arising out of its constriction is the Primal Light, or E which becomes the pure light of Being or Existence. The reduction of the Absolute into the emergent Light of E makes individuation possible. Thus the I (or individualized Light) becomes the stars in the sky, the countless fish in the sea, and all the creatures or the earth. water, and the air—including human beings. They are "legion" and represent the fragmentation of the Absolute into infinite parts for the sake of Being.

In order to communicate, the I reaches out to the not-I* and the play between these two generates the mortar needed for the recementing of the parts. Our self-awareness develops gradually. Metaphorically, it's as if the shrinkage of the A† into individual lights exposes the Absolute to the greatest possible risks, and shocks it into an awareness of its true predicament. The pruning, when done properly, stimulates new growth. The pruning of the Absolute is its abandonment to infinite selves, an utter dissolution for the

---

*It actually takes an incredibly long period of time before this distinction becomes clear. At the dawn of time, the seed of self was too immature to recognize the other, but now that it has germinated and developed, there is an opportunity for conscious reintegration.

†Compare this with the story of the jinni in the bottle, or the shrinkage of "god" into human form.

sake of consciousness. The twenty-six letters of the alphabet (which is the numeral value of the Hebrew *YHVH*, or God) constitute the differentiated elements of His Being. When they are taken together and reintegrated, the god is resurrected. Orpheus sings again, but this time a more lofty song.

Not only is the I connected to the You (as in the letter itself); but it also plays an essential role in denying it, because it senses the other as a threat to its own existence. This is an amazing paradox, because the essence of the I-Thou relationship furthers the evolutionary aims of humanity: when a single I mirrors the other, awareness can develop.

The stage for this drama is already set in the Five Vowels* as the Five Aspirations—what is humanly possible. Between the "I" and the "Thou" (U) lies the O, which holds the key to our transformation. For if we are to realize our Supreme Identity—that I=Thou=That or I Am that I Am (Tat Tvam Asi) it is essential that the being become as nothing (0). This is the Fairy Sword Bridge or the razor's edge that spans the asymptotal gap between I and Thou. One who accomplishes this transformation no longer says, on seeing an alien being, "There but for the grace of God go I," but rejoicing in their unity, exclaims, "There by the grace of God go I!"

The "body" of the language (the consonants) can be likened to a tire, and the vowels to the air (breath or spirit) that "animates" it. In the ancient Hebrew texts the vowels were not indicated but had to be supplied by the reader. This is an efficient means of preserving the sanctity of the original material, for the body could be stored up on library shelves, but not the life. That had to be reintroduced at each reading by the reader himself. In other words he had to pour his life into the body of the text for it to be re-animated, so that it would dance for him.

The numerical relationships of the vowels mirror my general thesis:

| | |
|---|---|
| A | 1st letter of the alphabet |
| E | 5th letter of the alphabet |
| I | 9th letter of the alphabet |
| O | 15th letter of the alphabet |
| U | 21st letter of the alphabet |

*The esoteric rendering of *vowel* is *vau-El*, or that which is joined (Vau) to God (El). As such, the vowel is the breath, bestower of life, the spirit of the Word.

Note that A + I ÷ 2 = E,  or  1 + 9 ÷ 2 = 5
And I + U ÷ 2 = O,  or  9 + 21 ÷ 2 = 15

This suggests that E and O are the halfway marks or balancing factors relating the A to the I and the I to the U. As such they register as "O" on the scale, serving as catalysts that transform A to I and I to U.

Equating the formless A to the "self-conscious" I is rendered possible through the mediation of the E, which can be likened to Desire: *the desire to be,* to have an organ of sight—an "I." Thus it is this intense concentration of the A transformed into the light of E (cf.*Eve,* which Qabbalistically can be rendered *Adam's desire to be*) that creates the condition for Original Seeing: an "I" that can look out on the world, and then, by reflecting back on itself, contemplate its own profundity.

In the case of the I and U nothing (O) really stands between them. There are no barriers (except illusory ones) to the realization of this identity. To break through this formidable illusion, the self must be reduced to *no-thing,* which then opens the way to the realization that I *am* Thou.

The first vowel (A) is seemingly the most abstract, while the last one (U) is seemingly the most removed from abstraction. It is man's "objective" world, perceived by the I as "you". To get from A to U one must learn to see both ways. This can be accomplished only with a balanced I, one that functions as fulcrum. In this capacity it realizes that it is simultaneously the Absolute I beholding itself and the I masquerading as a you in the mirror of the world.

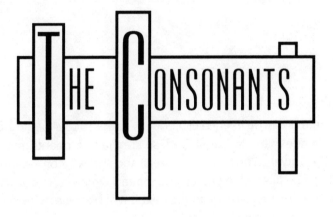

The consonants can be likened esoterically to the "body" of the alphabet. As we are made in the image of God, so are the consonants made in the image of the vowels. The "mind" (vowels) and "body" (consonants) of the alphabet can be likened to energy and matter, which can be equated. As we move from one consonant to the next it will become evident that this so-called "body" is really a "body of light."

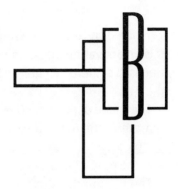

The letter B can be traced back to the second letter of the Hebrew alphabet, *Beth* (or house). The Old Testament opens with the letter B in Hebrew—*Bereshith** (in the beginning). Nor is this without design, for the A is too ineffable to begin.

B is a foundation letter, marking the emergence of life (cf. *bio*—life) and the *birth* of Man. Indeed, the letter B, only slightly modified, has become the word to express life: to *be*, or to exist.

The A then is the *not-to-be* (non-existence, or the ground of our being) out of which being arises. This B (as *Beth*) admirably describes our existence as the agency or vehicle that houses (Beth) the Lord (The Grand Aleph, or A).

Indeed, when the B is conjoined to the A, one Egyptian word for *soul* (*ba*) is generated. The ba is pictured as a bird with a human head to indicate the spirit (bird) taking on the form of Man (the A masquerading as the B).

When the A is joined to the B *Ab* is generated, which in the Egyptian language meant *heart*—a source of life. By the circumscription or limitation of A by B, life as we know it becomes possible. One might say that the A collapses in on itself in order *to be*. The B, then, is a binding power,

---

*Bereshith: in the "beginning" or in the *be-jinning*. That is to say, the enchantment, or the creation of maya.

generated by and impressing itself on the Almighty Aleph, or A. As such it is an activating force, an initial stirring of the Absolute; its first declaration is "Let there be light!" The A has built itself a house and had become the B.

The shape of the letter B roughly approximates two spheres and visually represents the initial division of the A. As *two* it makes for divided sight, but paradoxically that sight allows for depth perception. And so B generates the prefix *bi,* or *two.**

The B reminds us *to be,* that we are the embodiment of the mystery of manifestation, and that as gods we have taken on a particular form for this expression.

The *bee,* known for its activity (busy as a bee), is so named for the letter B, which is the beginning of all motion. One product of the bee's activity is honey, which represents the sweetness of being.

Among weavers, the word *abb* refers to the yarn used for the warp. By joining the A to the B, we can make a cover for ourselves a coat that will conceal our nakedness.

*Ab* used as prefix means from, separation, departure *(e.g. abscond, abduct, absolve).* There is an echo here of the primal division, the breaking up or the breaking away from the Source. There is also a paradoxical togetherness in the seeming separation. The A is still conjoined to the B, and together they express the power of the Word.

In *abba* (Aramaic for father—cf. *abbot)* there is the suggestion of "planter of the seed" so elegantly depicted in the conjoining of ab-ba. Thus the initial stirring that gave birth to infinite galaxies can be represented pictorially as a father who impregnated the Void.

*By,* meaning *next to, alongside,* or *around,* reflects not only the closeness of AB (spirit/body) but also its circumscription of all life.

As a woman becomes big with child, so the Aleph (A) swelled with the B, for by the act of retraction (Tsimtsum) it paradoxically became big unto bursting. And thus, qabbalistically speaking, there can be a "big bang" heralding the creation—a "*breaking* open," the *bursting* of a *bubble,* a

---

*Cf. the English word *both* with the Hebrew letter *Beth* (house). As the house is the home of the Spirit, the concept of two (both) is introduced. In a sense, then, these words are esoteric cognates.

*budding* and a subsequent *blooming*. From *Brahma* (the Creator) to *Buddha* (the enlightened one)!

Many other B words echo this process. Consider *baby*, for instance: the beginning of a human being. Then there are the "binding" words (the B as circumscriber), such as *boundary, band, brace, bark,* (binding a tree), *boa* (winding its coils), *bank* (binding the sea), *body* (binding the spirit), *bridle, boob* (hide bound), *betroth* (binding in marriage), *bake* (to bind by heat), *book* (words that are bound together), *belt, bar* (enclosing), *bolt* (joining or binding), *border, brink, brim, both* (two together), *bow* (referring to knot), *braid, brain* (that which coordinates or binds together the life of the body), *build, bundle, buckle, by* (near or beside—together), *bridge* (connecting), *bring* (the general sense of coming together).

Closely related to the concept of binding is the concept of swelling, bursting, birthing, as in *bud, bang, burst, bubble, bump, boss, bloom, built, big, big, bomb, ball, bell, belly, imbibe* (swell with drink), *Baal* (originally, fertility god), *bold, brash, blob, bloat, bread* (leavened), *brew, burn, breach, bray, break, bruise, brute*.

And since creation (to be) is often associated with the fall of man and therefore *evil* * (separation from the Source), the following B words reflect this state of being: *Bah!, bad, Baal, Beelzebub, boo!, bogy, bedlam, booby,* (due to the Lost Light), *boo-boo* (minor injury), *bane, baleful, bubonic* (from bubo), *Babel, beast, bum, batty, base* (ignoble), *barbaric, broken*.

---

*As usual, that which generates evil also generates life (evil is life reversed). Consider also the words *balm, best, beauty, bounty, beatific, bliss, bright, brilliant, bless,* etc.

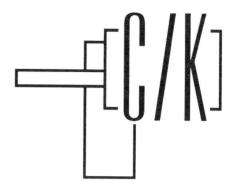

The A's self-imposed limitation, collapsing in upon itself in order to be (B)—to exist outside of itself—transforms into the C, a reborn and highly concentrated form representing the piercing power of A. This limitation of the light of *Aleph* paradoxically makes it visible and "C-ing" is made possible.

The sound of C can be concentrated (like light itself), as in *can* (K sound) or dispersed and softened as in *cell* (S sound). As the third letter of the alphabet it is neutral, with the power to expand itself (the letter S as a generator of plurals) and to mold (the K as molder, compressor).

The K actually looks like the C when the upright strike of the letter is removed ( |C ). Etymologically, it is related to the Hebrew letter *Kaph* (the hollow of the hand),* and, by extension, a mold. Thus the letter is related to shape: molding, containing, or holding. Consider, for example, such words as *keg, can* (noun), *cave, couch, cowl, coffin, casket, chalice, calix, calathus, cape, contain, case, canister, kiln, cell, cask, castle, cup, kylix, cap, canopy, keep, krater, cavity, kettle, church, kirk, car, coach, coronet, camera, caul, carton, caldron, cuspidor, crypt, cubby, cleft, crevice, cranny, cove, crate, cabinet, cabin, crucible, capsule, coffer, caddie, crib, caisson, cage, kit, corbeil, cradle, cask, kilderkin, canteen, cruse, carafe,*

---

*Note that the shape of C can also be likened to the hollow of the hand.

*cruet, caster, crock, cubicle, closet, commode, chiffonier, chest, chamber, corridor, kiosk, coif.*

As a consequence of molding, there is compressing, bringing together, compacting, hardening, as in *co* (as prefix—together with, joint), *kiss* (to press together), *echo** ("eko"—that which is compressed and bounced back), *kick, cute, ache* ("ak"—the pain of being compressed; cf. *Acheron*— Hades), *knock, nick, coke, cock, cook, cake, click, cliche* (from *klitsch*, meaning *clump*), *catch, come* (to bring together), *cast* (as in sculpture), *coil* (wind together), *call* (communication for the purpose of bringing together), *kill* (snuffing out), *Kali* (the Destroyer), *clunk, Cain* (smith, craftsman, a "compressor"), *crimp, crinkle, cramp, crooked, crinkum-crankum* (full of twists and turns).

Something compressed can become the source of great power and concealed light, as in *coal*. A *king* is a molder of men. When the word king is broken into its component parts, *K-ing* reveals that through the K-ing process a king is made. He is hewn or molded through *"kaphing"*; he is "hewmanized" (humanized), as it were, through pain and suffering. He who undergoes this initiation is worthy of becoming a king (cf. *khan* and *Cohen*, meaning priest). *Kith* and *kin* are friends and relatives (closeness). *Kinetic* is to move, press together (cf. *kindle*—to ignite by this friction). *Kin*, as suffix (cf. *lambkin*) is a diminutive, which illustrates the reducing or compressive power of K. In the suffix *icle* (as in *particle, icicle*) the force of K acts as diminutive (actually, in conjunction with the L).

The Egyptian *Ka* is the "double" (or soul) that survives the death of the body. As such it is the concentrated essence of a person. Esoterically, it is related to the Latin *qui* (who), which word also serves as a a name for the Supreme Diety (Who). In all probability Ki as "compressor" is associated with the interrogative pronoun *who* (qui) because it reflects the Almighty's ability to separate Himself from Himself, thus creating an archetypal mirror. As a consequence, God begins to "reflect"; He asks Himself, "Who am I?" But *Who* also represents the Grand Being who created the conditions for his own reflection: Who am I? I am Who! (Notice the construction of the question mark, collapsing in on itself, introspectively.)

---

*Cf. the dominant K in *economics*—the study of material wealth.

In the Far East *Ki* is the concentrated energy of life; to possess the *key* to something is to have the concentrated power to unlock it.

The K is the further involvement in manifestation of the C. The sound of C can sometimes be soft, as in *cell, cinder, cellar, and ceiling,* but the K is always hard. In this sense the C is an earlier form of the K, fluid, but underscoring the principle that if sight is not limited, narrowed or molded, "C-ing" is impossible.

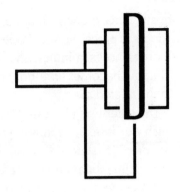

D, the fourth letter of the English alphabet, is derived from the Hebrew *Daleth* (or door), at once a separation or division from and a means of entering into. It brings into play the idea of threshold, or transition from one place or state of being to another. Therefore, as Fabre d'Olivet states in *The Hebraic Tongue Restored,* it also refers to nourishment—a *breast*—for to be on the threshold, poised to enter another state of being, is to position oneself to receive nourishment. The letter, D then can be seen as the Breast of our Provider. (Notice the shape of the letter D!)

To walk through this door is to enter the world of physical existence, the world of form,* where the quaternary† abounds. Because the world is experienced as divided or fragmented, the D also indicates division or separation. Consider, for example, the prefix *de* in such words as *derail, depilate, detach,* and *deform.*

D indicates descent (coming down)and refers to our passing through the threshold from a higher state (Paradise) to a lower one (the world of four, or the world of form), as shown in *destroy* (to cast down), *depress, decline, despise.*

This descent into the world and separation from Paradise is a kind of

---

*Cf. four—D is the fourth letter of the alphabet—to four-m/form.
†Cf. Tetragrammaton (YHVH) or the God of Four.

death. Since there is a fragmentation, and a separation, time begins. As the "doors of perception" are opened, the human being divides life into years, months, hours, minutes, and seconds.* The person becomes a dual being. The soul becomes time-bound—as in *di* (two or dual), in *dibasic,* and also in the related *dia.*

The letter D is also used to designate the past tense in thousands of English words (e.g., *captured, visited, did, died, made*). To say that someone has *died* is to state a *dis-continuity,* or separation. The life is over. It is past. (Recall that the prefix *de* means *to separate from,* and that the letter D itself is derived from *Daleth,* or a *door,* that divides one place or time from another.)

D connotes an overwhelming sense of *destruction, doom, death,* and *descent,* in the following words: *depth, despair, descend, decline, delve, deluge, dement, drat!, diggle, dybbuk, disaster, devastate, devil, demon, due, demise, deny, dreary, denounce, deplore, depress, drip, drop, drift, dry* (of the earth—solid—as opposed to heaven), *duck* (submerge), *destroy, destitute, desolate, dotage, drill, dig, demoralize, demi, demean, dis-* (as prefix—not), *dead, dread, dark, dangle, dive, dagger, deplete, defunct, defile, deflate, degrade, deficit, dip, decadent, debt, deep, deaf, daze, dino,* (terrible), *dys* (bad, evil, abnormal), *deceit, dirt, dire, drek, dull, dumb, difficult, deficient, damn, dope, droop, danger, dung,*† *dwarf, dwindle, dwine, drag, drugged, drown.*

Another key D word is *do,* for activity accompanies separation and fragmentation. Herein do the D and the B coincide.‡ Once the clock begins to

---

*How strange indeed that the second is the smallest conventional unit of time, as if to say that the primary unit is NOW which is beyond time.

†Cf. the child's words "doodoo" and "dooty." In my own family we coined the word (rather it presented itself from the deep unconscious) "dee-dee balls," as endearing a word for excrement as I have ever come across!

‡The B as the second letter and the D as the fourth also relate numerically. If B is squared, D is generated. Both letters are involved in manifestation, separation, and closing off. B to the third power generates H, once more an enclosing function (cf. the *Cheth,* or *fence*), and also self-activating. B to the fourth power generates the P, a very active letter. C squared generates I (the ninth letter). Both C and I are "seeing" letters. D squared generates P; both are active letters. The E squared generates the Y, which at the end of most words assumes the E sound.

tick there is movement, entropy, and eventually death. And so we have the word deed, a thing accomplished, or done.

In entering the World of Four (the earth)* one encounters the *devil, demons,* or *id*—all of which represent intense concentrations of energy and activity (cf. *deva, divine, deity—Demon est Deus inversus.*)

The word *dad* signifies the active partner (cf. *do*) in the male/female relationship. (The mom is the recipient—see the letter M). But the word curiously resembles *dead,* for behind all this activity, there is an additional requirement: *sacrifice.* The father gives up his seed to the world (mother) and in the act of doing so dies to the world to be resurrected through the child.† (It is intriguing that some male spiders are consumed by the female after copulation.)

The prefix *ad*‡ generally expresses *motion* toward (cf. *advance, admit*). In the modification *add,*§ it signifies increase, accretion, and the condensation of spirit into form (cf. the word *dew*). It is the way of manifestation, the way the day is born, for a day is a means of marking time or measuring motion. The D (or *day*) is the light that peers out of impenetrable darkness. (Cf. Lucifer as light bearer.) It represents potential activating itself.

---

*The ear-th is God's (Th-theos) "ear." In other words, the earth is the amplifier for that which we call God. Manifestation, then, is a way of drawing the Eternal Silence out of Itself, of making it speak (through a "personality," through a self— cf. the biblical "still small voice"). The earth is thus a musical instrument upon which the Sound of Unity can play its song.

†*Child* curiously sounds like "killed" if the Ch is pronounced as a K (as in Christ). Life (the child) and death (killed) are two ends of the same stick!

One possible "esoteric" rendering of *Adam,* (the Primal Man): *towards* (ad) *being* (am). In other words, Adam/Eve moves towards being or existence and life in the world. Consider the names *Adam* and *Eve,* which can be modified to read Odd-am and Eve-n (odd and even) or the generation of all possible numbers—the multitudes. That which is *odd* is "angular" (indeed, odd is derived from a word originally meaning point of land, triangle), which lends itself to the D formation— the barb or sting of manifestation! (as opposed to the "even" homogeneity of the Spirit or non-manifested state).

§Cf. *aid*—help, assistance—"increase."

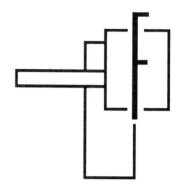

The sixth letter of the English alphabet, F, is derived from the Hebrew *Vau* (nail). It is clearly related to the letter V and even assumes its sound in the formation of many plurals (e.g. loaf to loaves). Consider also, in this connection, the preposition *of,*\* which often means "connected with" as in "Robin Hood *of* Sherwood Forest."

This joining function of the F is evident in many words: *file* (to arrange together), *feel* (connect with), *fuse, fit, fetch, form, fetter, fiancé* (joined by vow), *fagot* and *fasces* (both bundles of sticks), *fascia* (connective tissue), *fasten; fay* (as verb—to fit closely or exactly, to join), *female* (joined to the male), *family, faith* (joined to the Source), *fate* (that which binds), *forge* (to join), *fillet* (narrow band to fasten the hair), *federate, firm* (joined together), *fiscal* (derived from a root meaning "to weave," "to tie"), *affiliate, fix, focus* (come together), *fold* (as verb), *fuck, fornicate, fertile, fecund, fetus, friend, fist* (clenched fingers).

The word *if* is a good example of how the F fuses or joins. Grammatically, it introduces a condition or contingency: "*If* you will listen, then you will hear," The moment one hears "if," another idea is expected to follow—to "join" with it.

The F generates a related series of words: *fight, fury, foe, fit* (as related

---

\*Cf. *off*—"not joined"—the linguistic phenomenon of the generation of opposites.

to violence), *feisty, feint, ferment, fervor, fervent, fervid, feud, fiery, fission, fierce, fiendish, foment, flail, flagrant, foray, flagellate, flagitious, flare, flash, fleece* (as verb), *flay, fracas, fray, frighten, and frenzy.* Generally speaking, these words either clash with a foe or move passionately toward a friend or ideal. Here the joining speaks more of combat or religious fervor.

Since the F is a fricative, the sound it emits can be likened to a narrow stream of wind. Thus the sound F also generates words with an onomatopoetic feeling: *fly, fart, fill, fool,* (from *follis*—bag of wind), *folly* (empty wind), *fad* (a superficial wind, something that fizzes), *fade, fan, feather, flow, flutter, fugue, fife.*

The force of F can also become diminished in such words as *feeble, faint, flag* (verb), *flaccid, flabby, fail, fall, flop, fizz, famine, falter, fatigue, frozen, frigid, fade, -fid* (as combining form—split apart), *friction.**

To be *free* seems to imply non-involvement, freedom from all connections. But paradoxically, to be free is to be joined to one's God, to be at one with Him. Christ is free, yet he utters "I and my Father are one."

*Four,* as related to the world of *form,* is most likely connected to the Tetragrammaton in its relationship to the *mercavah* (vehicle). In more familiar terms it is the relationship between soul and body. Why should a world materialize? What purpose (if any) does it serve? What is it *for?* Qabbalistically *four* can be reduced to FR or the penetrating power (F) of the will (R). It poses something of a universal koan: How can the Great Spirit (Jinni) enter into King Solomon's bottle, then be cast into the sea (of maya) and still be free (FR)?†

To understand the nature of this equivalency (Tat Tvam Asi), the equivalency of the limitless taking on our limits, or a crucified Christ fully joined to his Father in heaven, is to understand all that free (FR) means—or what a man is living *for?*

To have good "for-tune" is to be in *tune* with *for* (or the world of four), which is "square"‡ as opposed to the spirit assuming the form of a circle which has "no beginning and no end."

---

*Friction is created by the opposition of joining—the basic sense of F (or *Vau*).
†This is the kenosis of Christ, the humbling process of being born as man.
‡Cf. the "four corners" of the world.

Movement may create the illusion of freedom, but how often do we drag our internalized chains along with us even after we become aware of them! In this sense even a slave can be free while the master may still be in bondage. Ice is only less free than steam if one defines freedom as "vapor." To be free, in a more profound sense, is to realize that the center is no greater than the circumference. It is to realize that spirit is equal to the body and that one is equivalent to the other. In other words, what seems very small (the body) is truly equivalent to that which is very limitless (the spirit).

To be truly *free* is to be identified with the whole not with the part. To be identified with the whole enables one to fully enter the part (the bottle) as if it were the whole, for in essence it is! The free person realizes that there are no parts and so can abandon the self to the play of life in any form it may take. A free man has nowhere to go, for he is everywhere. He can be all things to all men. But this is realized only after long exposure to life with all its sufferings and joys.

The F makes it possible for us to nail or join ourselves to the cross (where time and eternity meet). Only in this way (kenosis) can we experience our freedom in its most debased form. This is the *crisis* (cf. Christ) we undergo as human beings. To be able to will (R) our own death on the cross is to be able to realize that in owning nothing we own all.

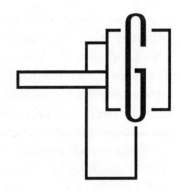

The English letter G is related to the Hebrew letter *Gimel* (camel or throat). In a broad sense these two images are conveyors.

The letter G resembles a C moving into itself or turning toward itself. (Some scholars trace the shape of C to a boomerang.) It suggests a universal need to form a passageway or conveyor, to make a gut, womb, or hollow that closes in on itself in order to digest or reproduce. (Cf. the word *egg* and the embryonic shape of the letter *G*.) The sound of G is guttural, originating in the depths of the body *(goo, gulch, gunk, gob, glut, glue, gullet, guzzle).*

As "conveyor" the G is closely associated with movement: *go, get, gust, ghost* (spirit wind), *god* (prime mover), *gas, gig, glib, gush, goad, gabble, gadfly, gain, gait, goal* (movement toward), *gale, gallop; gambol, game, gam* (the leg as instrument of movement), *gangway, gauntlet, garrulous, gerund, geste, gesture, glide, gibber, gazelle, gavotte, give.*

The movement can also become sluggish, completely bound up with itself, as in *gag, gel, gunk, goo, lag, gum, gasp, gawky, glue, gley, glob, gluten, gook, guck, goop, galoot, gangrene* (obstruction), *gaol,* (confinement), *grume.*

*Grrr,* as expressed by an aroused animal, warns the intruder of a deep, inner stirring (G) that could be thrust outward (R) to meet any threat. Likewise, the word *ugh* is an onomatopoetic expression of inner disgust pushed outward—a gut-level reaction.

In the word *god,* the G stands for organic transformation. This process of turning in on itself (like a serpent feeding on its own tail) is an excellent visual symbol of the deity undergoing evolution along with his creation. The esoteric meaning of the D reinforces the visual symbol of the G and suggests that the mysterious transformation of death is made possible only through a reciprocal process of consuming and dying. What goes into the gut is transformed into a higher level of existence. In moving toward death evolution is made possible, and one who accomplishes this feat achieves the status of a god. The middle O represents the center or nothing (O)—that which has no face, form, or figure. To realize that the transformation of life into death, and therefore death into life (GD), is made possible through the intermediary of the spirit (O), where nothing is really lost and nothing is really gained, is to know and understand the sacred name of God.

The wonder of it all can be expressed by the exclamation *gee!* For what can be a greater miracle than the miracle of transformation, a miraculous consuming of oneself to nourish the spirit?

But why does the mere reversal of God change it into *dog?* How can the idea of God, so lofty in conception, be reduced to dog, the symbolic "other end" of the spectrum? (Cf. "My dogs—*feet*—hurt"). It can be approached esoterically on two levels—from the point of view of what a dog stands for symbolically, and from an analysis of the sound of DG.

In the role of guard, the dog is an excellent symbol for the mind, which also guards (cf. *mind,* meaning *"to watch"*). The concept of mind as guardian is quite simple to grasp, when we consider the role the mind plays in protecting us; for without a mind and the power to reflect, we would fall prey to countless alien forces that would soon destroy all our possibilities for evolution. The Dog as symbol, therefore, relates closely to the idea of God.

Dogs representing feet makes even more sense in this connection, because the feet are basic: we stand on them. They give us stability. We are based in God, He is thus our under-*standing.* The wild dog has become gentle in his association with man, the mighty power of the universe—God—subject to the taming or timing powers, has also been channeled into serving the evolving mind of man.

The DG as in *dig, dug*—even *dagger*—penetrates. Madame Blavatsky was fond of the expression "Fohat (creative force) digs holes in space." The

D as *Daleth,* a door or a "hole in space," followed by the G as *Gimel,* or organic movement, expresses just this descent of the Spirit and its involvement in its own creation, The DG also represents the desire to dig in or manifest. Thus GD and DG are two sides of the same coin: one side is lofty and spirit-like whereas the reverse is concrete, but in the midst of that mysterious substance dwells the living God.

The word *gold* (earth light) is also constructed to reflect the wonder of organic transformation. The alchemists sought to make gold out of lead or some other base substance. Although this is theoretically possible, the gold of the real alchemists was the gold of transformation. It is their dream that the dross within them should be raised up and transformed into gold to light up their lives. The G represents this transformation process. The letter O is the realization that the self (ego) has to be sacrificed—become as nothing. In this way death (the D or lead) is overcome and raised up to the level of L, (El Elohim or creator gods).The *gold* of the alchemist, then, is death and resurrection of the spirit through organic transformation, and it is this that makes a person glow.

This re-birth of the golden light can be expressed in many other G words, including *glow, glint, glabrous* (smooth, reflecting light), *glare, glaze, gleam, glimmer, glass, glisten, glad, glitter, gloaming, gloss, glacé.* Since light can be more or less intense, the word *gloom* is positioned along the lower end of this gradient.

The turning in of the letter G toward itself in a process of organic transformation is reflected in many "enclosing" words, for instance, *guard* (to surround), *gizzard, girth, girdle, gyrate, gyre, garrote, garter, grasp, gasket, gastro-, gather, gland, grommet, glove, Gaea* and *geo* (earth), *garland, gestalt, gastrula, -gon* (suffix meaning "angle"—as in *polygon,* which derives from a root meaning "bent" or "crooked"—or that which encloses), *grail, gut, grotto, gullet, guzzle, gully, grave, gorge, gate* (opening).

Because this womb-like enclosing is generative, serving as a vehicle for transformation, the following words are G-oriented: *gonad, gentle* (of noble birth), *germinate, gestation, genuine* (pure bred), *gender, gall* (digesting fat), *gyno, genital, groin, gorgon* (transformed to stone), *-gony* (as suffix—something generated), *golem* (derived from a word meaning *embryo*).

The magnitude of the G-process, which gives birth to worlds upon worlds and can transform a mustard seed "which indeed is the least of all seeds:

but when it is grown, it is the greatest among herbs. . . "(Matt. 13:32), is illustrated by the following words: *great, giant, grand, gain, God, gorilla, grow, age* (the aging process, transformation), *glut, gross, googol,\* gargantuan, Gog* (high mountain), *galaxy, goliath.*

The G-process has not only a bright but also a severe aspect, as is reflected in the following words: *grim, grimace, grunt, grumble, grump, grouch, grime, ghastly, grief, grind, grisly, grist, grueling, gruff, grudge, gripe.* Man is that peculiar animal capable of giving birth to grumps on the one hand and "gubbies" on the other, and it seems that the right hand never knows what the left hand is doing!

---

*Googol is described by the dictionary as an arbitrarily coined word. It was first introduced by the mathematician Edward Kasner, whose son, on seeing a very large number 1 followed by a hundred zeros, uttered "googol!" But it is not arbitrary at all, as children have a way of being in touch with the archetypes of the language. Understanding intuitively that G-words tend to express bigness and greatness, Kasner's son came up with a marvelously descriptive word! As a child I called my mother *guggie,* instinctively understanding that the G wraps around itself and that *guggie* expressed my love for a most wonderful human being. It was an instinctive hug. My own wife, knowing nothing about this coinage of mine, called our own children *gubbies.* This is no "chance" word. On the contrary *googol, guggie,* and *gubbie* are instinctively born of the font that generates our language.

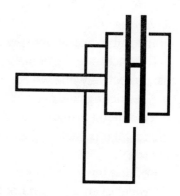

The eighth letter of the English alphabet, H, derives from the Hebrew *Cheth* (fence). It symbolizes the self (personality) but also the greater Self. At once the H is the "fenced in" man* (limited, mortal), and the Oversoul.† Strange bedfellows!

Although the H is double-aspected, reflecting both the self and the Oversoul, the dominant influence is that of *Cheth*. A fence encloses a space to individuate it so that a certain work can be done; this includes the work of making a man—as self. Thus the H has come to stand for the self in all its pettiness and in all its grandeur. It is the individuating faculty in man, that devil in him that leads him on to cultivate his own garden, if need be at the expense of his neighbor—who lives on the other side of his "fence!"

This individuation process (H-ing) is important because it concentrates the life energies in the cultivation of a specific portion of land. It is symbolized by the sacred enclosure (*temenos*) within which the farmer plants the seed. This self-limitation develops will, which is represented pictori-

---

*Note that the English H, when connected in series, is also a "fence" (┼┼┼┼┼). The Egyptian hieroglyph for this aspect of the H was a rope twisted into a figure 8. (Note the near equivalency of sound of the letter H (*eight-ch*) to the number *eight*.)

†The life itself is attributed to *Heh* (window) the fifth letter of the Hebrew alphabet (a breath of fresh air).

ally by the unicorn standing in the center of the enclosed garden. (The single horn symbolizes a unified will, one that pierces the veil of maya.)

This enclosure, the domain of self, is what we possess and what possesses us, protective while we are developing but after a critical point, confining, restricting, and even killing us.

It is difficult to understand the self, because like the Lord Himself (or the life force) it is "nearer than our hands and feet," therefore we simply do not see it.

Because the self fences in, it also cuts off, and in so doing, incorporates. Consider even the sound of the letter H: "ate-ch." It is the sound of the serpent consuming ("ate-ching") its own tail. (Cf. the shape of the number 8, which when not completely closed suggests a bending back on the self for self-consumption ( $\delta$ .) That is the secret of H: it has to be eaten. The only way to liberate the life force is to consume it. This concept can be seen in the word *hate* (h-ate), which contains its own antidote, for to transcend hate, to overcome it, is to consume (ate) the self (H): h-ate. Unfortunately, however, most human beings hate so hard and so much that they want to consume "the other" and tear him apart, having forgotten that the hate born of wisdom is to hate the hate!

In this enclosure of self (H—the rock to which man is chained) the work at hand is to perfect the man, which when brought to the point of perfection sacrifices his life to the greater Self (Heh). And so God sent His beloved Son—*as sacrifice!* This sacrifice, if it is to be effective, must be nearly perfect, virtually without flaw. We suffer because we do not want to give up our accomplishments. "My time has not come," we lament. Surely Abraham did not want to sacrifice Isaac, his near-perfect, most beloved son. But that is what is required of the Son of Man, Abraham, and all of us. The self must be sacrificed, not by an outside force but by our own hands. (It was Christ, after all, who directed the drama of the crucifixion, although it seemed to happen on the outside.) To accomplish this extremely difficult task, human beings must rise higher than the angels, for we are defined as creatures who have the potential to give up everything—to sacrifice all for the sake of All.

As cultivators of mind substance we eat the fruit of our own labor, the most precious food of all being—the self. Indeed, the most excellent meal for man *is* man. He is that noble cannibal whose higher Self devours the lower, and so he assumes the shape of the serpent eating its own tail until all is consumed but the "I" (Heh, or life).

In the overall design of Nature, then, the self was meant to be consumed along with other food, instead it feeds on its host. That is the essential reason why we become possessed.

How is this reflected in the hundreds of H words? As a fragrance or a savor which one has to sniff out.*

The essence of H is limitation. It is concentration of mind substance so that a seed can be planted and a certain work accomplished. Thus it implies narrowing down, enclosing, grasping. Everything comes to a *head*. There is an impact, as with a *hammer*. Something is *hit*. There is *heaviness, horniness, hardness, harshness.* This concentration generates a great *heat* (cf. *hot*). The effort is *here* (cf. *to hear,* which originates from the concept of being on one's guard, being attentive—being *here*). A *hero* is someone who can be here, now, who has overcome all distractions. His mind is concentrated. He is a hero and therefore at the *helm*. Esoterically, this stems from the concept of individuation (H).

Another meaning of limitation is to impede movement, as in *hobble, hamper, horrify* (transfix), *hesitate (hem* and *haw), hack.* The impeded movement may slow down even more, as in *hang, hold, heave,* (Indo-European base: to seize, grasp), *hawk* (grasping claws), *hinge, hoard, hook, hitched, Harpy* (snatcher), *handle* (something to hold onto), *hilt, haft, heed, hawser, harness, havoc,*(base: to seize), *hell* (where one is "bound"), *habit* (tending to "bind" one, either by clothes or in an emotional way), *have* (possess), *hag* (originally a witch (earthbound), *halt, hamper, hasp, heavy, hebetate, hedge* (to hedge in), *helotry* (slavery), *hermetic* (sealed), *hex* (to stop the flow, impede the life, bring bad luck), a *hog* (grasping), *home* (basic sense: to lie down, rest), *hurdle, hush, hypno-.*

Impeded movement tends to fold back on itself, as in a *helix, helminth,*

---

*This is true of all the letters. Corruptions and distortions of one sort or another alter the original intent of the elemental signs that compose it. Add to this the linguistic phenomenon of "generation of opposites" and one realizes how difficult it is to understand the shades of meaning each letter can assume in any one word. Also, the position of each letter in the word is important, for other letters can also affect its meaning.

*hem, hank, hock, hoop, hook, heart, holo* (circling back), *horizon* (bounding circle), and *hub.*

Limitation, involving a fencing in, also implies a cutting off or severing from the Source (cf. *hem, hemi* [a folding back], *half*) Man digs a *hole* in space, which becomes his sacred enclosure or field of work. This "falling" (cutting off) can be likened to a *hewing* (cutting out). The word *hay* also stems from the idea of cutting (cut grass). *Hoe* also derives from a word meaning "to cut." (In this connection compare the word hog—a castrated boar.)

The severe trauma of this "cutting off" (cf. the primordial cutting off, or the "fall of man") generates *havoc, hazard, harm, hurt, hassle, harass, heckle, hiss* (to frighten someone away), *hectic, hostile, heinous, horror, hell, Hades, hideous, haggard, hermit* (cut off).

Self-enclosure creates the concept of territory or possession, as reflected in *have, haven, home, his, her, habit, hug* (to hold close, possess), *hall, hollow, hallowed, halo, hat, harbor, hood, haunt, hauberk, helmet, heed.*

When life is liberated from the form (*Heh* as opposed to *Cheth*), the following words can be cited as examples: *helio* (sun), *hemo* (blood), *happy* (of the spirit), *halo, hop, hope, hi!* (life!), *high* (elevated or aspiration), *ah!* (wonder), *He* (life itself, referring to God), *hover, ho! hie, hepatic, hurrah, how!* (as greeting), and *hue.*

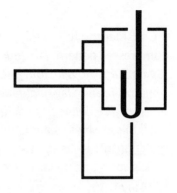

The J, which follows the I in the English alphabet, is also related to it historically. Both are offshoots of the same concept, the J separating into the consonantal branch and the I serving as vowel. As "body" the J can be considered as an I rooted in manifestation. Even the shape of the J suggests the sending out of roots to accommodate the "frozen light" in matter. The sound of J corresponds to the soft G, and when these two letters are drawn back to back they are mirror images of each other (ᘺᘺ) symbolizing corporeal involvement, as in the name *Jesus*.

The J expresses greater depth of penetration into matter than the I. Its shape suggests that it can get "hooked" into more objects and caught on to more things than the I. In the essence, it is a pent-up I, compressed into a "cubicle" and ready to spring up like a jack-in-the-box. Compare the idea of the jack in that toy, which *jumps* out at you, with an automobile *jack*, which also makes something jump up. Apple*jack*, gives one a needed lift! The J begins the word *jumpy*, it's a compressed I attempting to straighten itself out.* It reflects the agitation and commotion caused by being squeezed or confined to a limited space.

---

*In the game of jacks the pebbles or jacks are tossed up. Jack, in addition, means male, usually the more active member of the species, as opposed to the receptive female. Jack also means large or strong, for to withstand such pressure (as the compressed I or J), one either collapses or develops greater strength.

Consider the following J words, which illustrate the jumpy, agitated, compressed pattern: *jab, jerk, jangle, jar* (as verb), *jilt, jangle, jumble, jinx juggle, jump, joggle, jolt, jostle, judder, jig, jink, jog, jabber, jiggle, jitters, jimjams, jigsaw, jag, jactitation, javelin, jimmy* (verb), *jam* (verb), *jetsam, jettison, jibe, jet, jeer, junk* (thrown out), *jeté, jilt, jockey, jail* (confine).

All this evolves esoterically from the "casting out" of the I and its transmutation into J—its abandonment, confinement, and consequent agitation.

This springing up, as in *jack,** also generates such words as *joy* (raised spirits), *jaunty, jazz, jolly, jovial, juicy* (lively, spirited), *jee* (a variant of gee, expressing wonder), *jeepers* (surprise, wonder), *jester, Jesus* (lifting the Spirit), *jingo!* (exclamation indicating strong assertion or surprise), *Jehovah, jewel, joke* (that which raises our spirit).

The other side of J is the confinement of the I, its burial, which generates the word *jail* or "j-ail"—the confinement of "ail," El, or God. It also generates *jewel* (cf. diamond)—that which is found at the "center" of the earth, where it has been compressed for eons. *Jaw* is that which holds tight, grasps. To *jell* is to take form, to crystallize. *Join* (as in yoke) is meeting, mating, or compounding. The word *joke* (related to *yoke*) is generated in this context by entrapment in a tight spot, in which one's essence is bared. In other words, the biggest and best joke of all is that Man, an infinitely expansive spirit, universal in the scope and breadth of his conception, is confined (like the *jinni* in the bottle) to a *jot,* trapped in a limited, mortal form—yoked to it. Like the ox, grand symbol of sacrifice, he uses this predicament to plow the land and make it fertile. It reminds one of the reply the crucified man gave when asked if it hurt. "Only when I laugh," he said. Only a very great soul, the soul of man, can humble himself to such an extent that he is capable of laughing at such jokes!

The word *law* (cf. *jus, just, justice*) is also "J" oriented. It is the law of our life to be confined. (Cf. the law, as a body of regulations that aims to control the zigzag "jumpy" movements of Man. Also, the word *law* reversed generates *wal-l*—that which confines or limits.)

*Job,* as the archetypal man, underwent intense suffering (like Prometheus) for the sake of "lowering his sights" or transforming his all-seeing eye (I) into the imprisoned J. Man's *job* on earth is to effect this transformation.

---

*It's such a rich word! Think of Jack be nimble, Jack be quick, Jack jumped over the candlestick! And, of course, Jack the Giant Killer, who climbed—jumped up—the beanstalk. Jack also means *knave*—he "jumps" at you!

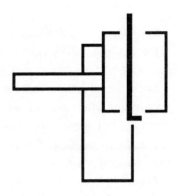

The twelfth letter of the English alphabet, L, can be traced back to the Hebrew *Lamed* (ox-goad). It is a letter that moves in low and high places (its shape suggests vertical and horizontal thrusts). As it wanders throughout the lower world it presents the following words: *low, lie, let* (to hinder), *left* (from weak), *load* (noun), *lady* (female, earthy), *languid, elf, lee* (a shelter), *latch, lag, lame, loll, lull, leak, labor, lapse, lose, louse, lout, law* (from laid down), *lees* (dregs), *less, ill, lead* (the metal), *Lethe, lapse, lame, little, fell, limit, lethargy, locked, kill* (lay down), *languor, leave, leaf* (that which falls), *lump*. (As suffix, *le* can mean "small"—as in *icicle*.)

On the vertical branch it is more open, vaulting to heaven, as in *laugh, lilt, leonine, lark, lily* (symbol of purity), *limpid, light, Allah, Eli* (meaning high), *Lord, all, lux, lift, lofty, elate, elope* (from "to leap up"), *lavish, levity, lusty, elevate, love, leap.*

Since the L reaches the highest and the lowest, extending itself in both directions, it may be said that its most basic characteristic is extension. (Hieroglyphically, the L is not only an ox-goad but also an extended hand. Consider the following words: *line, lane, limb, leg, long, list, lead* (verb), *log, ladder, label, lance, land, lanky, lasso, lateral* (to spread out), *latten, lattice, lath, launch, lawn, lea, leaf* (flat, thin, expanded organ), *leash, ledge, length, latitude, elastic, elapse, ell* (a measure of length), *else* (from a root meaning "that, yonder one."

In pronouncing the letter L, the tongue must turn back on itself to produce a rolling sound. Thus the high and low aspects of the L can be marked off on a circle (cf. *limbo, link, liaison,* where the L is neither here nor there).

Symbolically, the L can be seen as the Lord God Himself asleep in his profundity. The ox-goad, which the L resembles, prods Him to wake up, often against enormous odds.

The definite article *the,* in French, becomes *le* or *la; le garcon* (the boy) enriches the noun with the graciousness of L, which in its highest aspect is God.*

The idea of *le* as definite article is carried over into English in another aspect. As a suffix, *le* refers to a person who does something specific (as in *beadle*) or an object put to a specific use (as in *girdle, handle*). It is the same concept: the Most High El (Allah) graces every specific thing. Nothing is excluded from the attention of the Lord.

*Le,* as suffix, also indicates frequency, as in babble, prattle, prickle. That is, the action is continued or repeated (cf. *prick* to *prickle*), which is characteristic of the L's power of *extension* or movement in all directions.

---

*In English *the* boy is equivalent to saying, The(os) boy. Thus we are joined to our highest principle.

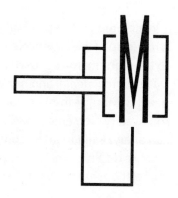

The thirteenth letter of the English alphabet, M, is derived from the Hebrew *Mem* (water). The English M still retains the hieroglyphic form of waves (∧∧∧∧). Mythologically, water symbolizes the mother* out of which the sun and all life arise (cf. Aphrodite, the goddess of love, who sprang from the foam of the sea).

The word Mom, and the expression for delight—mmmmmmm!—echo the joy of this life-giving water. Water is a receptive substance, and as such symbolizes the woman as earth mother, the receptacle of the seed. *Me,* as the objective case of *I* (also *my* and *mine*), is the receiver as opposed to the bestower of gifts, the more active I. This is clearly indicated in the expression I AM, wherein the I is active and the AM† the ground from which the I emerges.

When I is placed directly in the center of *am,* it generates the word *aim.* In esoteric terms, then, we should aim at centering our I in the ground of our being (am). We should always be balanced at the center point.

---

*Merely invert the W and *water* is magically transformed into the Latin word for mother, *mater.*

†AM reversed is MA, or Mother, the ground of our being or "amness." Thus M, as mother, is also M for the ground of our being, symbolizing manifestation and earthly life. Consider the M words *matter, mortal, matrix, mind,* and *maya.*

Water, the prototype of all mirrors, reflects or *mimics*. The word *mime* is made up of the watery element, which reflects or mimics all things. And so the word mem-ory, that which reflects the original light.*

The words *mental* and *mind* are constructed with an initial M to emphasize that Man, as thinker, could not develop if his makeup did not contain soft, watery elements. As Man, he is the mirror of manifestation, a lens that can analyze life in all its component parts.

Fabre d'Olivet, in *The Hebraic Tongue Restored,* observes an interesting relationship between the words *water* and *what:*

> . . . from the Chinese to the Celts all peoples may draw from the word which, in their tongues designates water, the one which serves as indeterminate pronominal relation. The Chinese say *choui,* water and *choui,* who, what? The Hebrew *Mah* or *Mi,* water and *Mah* or *Mi,* who, what? The Latins, *aqua,* water, and *quis, quae, quod,* who, what? The Teutons and Saxons, *wasser, water,* and *was* or *-wat,* who, what? . . . (p. 42 of the section entitled *Cosmogony of Moses.*)

Why this curious relationship? D'Olivet does not venture to say, but esoterically it is likely to have come about because water is the primal reflecting medium, and Man (composed of over seventy percent water) is the primal "reflecting" (thinking) medium. In reflecting, he is wont to ask himself *"who, what?"* in a way reminiscent of the ancient mirror of our being, the waters of Maya.

Water, as the universal solvent,† wears down all manifested life. Paradoxically, what has come to symbolize life, refreshing and nourishing it,

---

*Mem-or-y,* or the waters (*Mem*) reflecting the light of the sun (*or, aurum*—gold and aura—halo; consider also the word ore, the bedrock of metals, and the elements of the sun). Therefore our memories can be seen as "watery slates" reflecting the images of life, poetically rendered as the "or" or golden sun. Consider, in this connection, the word *more* (m-ore)—the multiple images or the multiple objects of manifestation (maya) generated by reflected light (aurora).

†Consider also the curious word *absolute* (the first principle, God), which esoterically (if not etymologically) is a construct of *ab* (father) and *solute* (that which is dissolved). That is, the Primal Father, the Planter of Seeds is dissolved in his manifestation. This echoes the creation myths in which God is fragmented into many parts and is dissolved in the world. Man has to rise out of the waters, just as the god Osiris was resurrected after the fragments of his body were cast into the Nile.

can also break it down* into a more undifferentiated state. Thus the "mother" is seen not only as beneficent but also as destructive—the terrible stepmother in fairy tales.

The two other common states of water, steam and ice, suggest that water is basically "three" (note the chemical formula; HOH), and that life, as symbolized by the water, moves in two directions—towards steam, a gaseous or spiritualized element, and towards ice, the frozen waters of manifestation, where stasis makes it difficult to stir the mind.

The word *mum* (closure, silence) connotes the closed, locked-up aspect of manifestation and also the enveloping womb of the mother. So also with *mummy* (an embalmed body), at once the death-like or frozen aspect of life in this world and at the same time the womb for the spirit's transit to the next world. Even the sound of M, a voiced bilabial nasal, invokes closure.†

---

*Cf. *Maim, mal, maul* (as verb), *malign, mad* (mental illness), *mold* (relating to decay-causing fungi), *mis-* (as prefix—wrong, bad), *moan, molest, macerate.*
†Cf. *aum (om)* a sound that encompasses the most open A to the closed-off M. That is, the sound of God includes the entire spectrum of life.

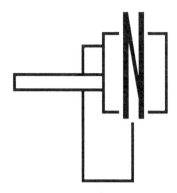

The N, or fourteenth letter of the English alphabet, derives from the Hebrew *Nun* (fish). Fish are the eyes of the sea. Indeed, the shape of a fish (⬥⬥)
is similar to the shape of the eye (⬥). The N represents the spirit* hidden
within manifestation. (Structurally, the letter N is hidden within the M!)†
Since the spirit is elusive, evading the material and moving toward the immaterial (nothing), the N generates a host of negative words such as *none,
nothing, never, nil, not, no, night, negative, un-, in-* (as in *inability), nill,
need, null, naught, nix, nadir, naked, ninny, nag, nay, nano* (very little),
*nap* (to sleep, less conscious), *narco-* (stupor), *narrow* (moving toward nothing), *nasty, nefarious, neglect, neither, needle* (narrowed), *nemato-* (thread-
like), *Nemesis, nether, nihil, niggard, nullity, nycti-, eon* (time moving toward eternity or nothing).

No moral judgment is intended here, as the N merely describes a state
of being. For example, *narco-* (sleep, stupor) moves toward a constricted
state of consciousness, *negating* the waking state.

The qabbalistic *Ain* (meaning Nothing) describes a state of non-being
which is beyond God and incomprehensible to man. It is my belief that
esoterically the slang word *ain't* is derived from it!

---

*Cf. *ion* (a charged atomic particle, the vital principle itself).
†The M is an N with an extra "root" thrown down to anchor it in manifestation.

Actually, the N moves in both directions. As a spirit letter it is also ever renewing, bubbling up from the source of our being (No Thing). In this respect, consider the following words: *new, neo, now, natal, navel, net, nave, ness, nine* (source of renewal or birth). In *nun* it describes a woman who has renewed herself through renunciation.

*In* refers to interior, an appropriate designation for the letter N, while *on* implies contact (the book is *on* the table), descriptive of the pervasive presence of N whether visible or invisible. If the light is *on*, there is also contact with a source (in this instance, electricity), but if it is *off* (not *on* or *no*, the reverse of *on*), the spirit has withdrawn from it. A ninny is a nonentity, a being who is "nothing." After nine the numbers begin again; they renew themselves. Likewise, in the ninth month the baby is born and time or the numbers begin again!*

The word *Man* is composed of three letters. The central A is the bridge between manifested (M) and unmanifested (N) life. In his midst is the A, that Grand Principle that lends itself to all aspects of life, manifested and unmanifested alike.

When reversed, the word *man* forms the root for *nam-e,*† for man inscribes his name on all things, and the names he invents are different aspects of the generic name, *man.*

The entire alphabet pivots around the M and N. M is the thirteenth letter counting forward, whereas N is the thirteenth letter counting backward. In their midst is the A, or First Principle. So man is concealed in the midst of the Word (alphabet) and is responsible for balancing it.

---

*Nine actually consumes itself as *Teth:* the ninth letter of the Hebrew alphabet, signifying a serpent, eats its own tail. (Note the shape of the letter Teth ( **ᕙ** ): when the serpent consumes itself the end result is *nothing* (N), *ninny, nine*—cf. *nein.*)

†The word *name* itself, when reversed, spells *eman*, the root of *emanate*. The suggestion is that names are emanations of that central sun, the spiritualized man. To name something is to know its essence, and this is a very high calling. Thus the name of an animal—say a lion describes certain leonine qualities, and the name *lamb* describes (among other things) gentle ones—all reflected in Man. There is not one named entity appearing on the outside of man that is not inside of man himself, the very creature who named the other creatures. So in classifying the world according to kingdom—animal, vegetable, mineral—man is describing the different elements of his being.

Consider the following MN words as related to balance: *mean* (middle or average), *mind* (serving as ballast). *Moan* is of particular interest, for the moan of pain is an instinctive attempt to restore balance. The sound of a moan, *ommmmmm,* is an unconscious uttering of the universal sound of God (Aum), through which one attempts to reestablish equilibrium. Other balancing MN words are *main* (central), *mend* (to make whole, restore to balance), *mine* (referring to "me," the center of my universe), *mint* (new, all there, still together), *mono* (one, unified), *monad* (indivisible unit), *moon* (an organism that plays an important role in balancing and centering the earth), *money* (a medium of exchange which ideally equates price with value), *mantra* (hymn or prayer that can restore or maintain balance).

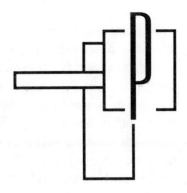

P, the sixteenth letter of the English alphabet, is derived from the Hebrew *Pe* (mouth). The mouth, as organ of speech,* is man's golden attribute, through which he reaches out to, and communicates with, his fellow human beings.

The articulation of an interior sound (the Voice of the Silence), and its movement outward into the world where it falls on receptive ears, are associated symbolically with "extension," or the male: that aspect of the human being that plants the seed.

Consider, for example, the words *pop, pope,* and *pa.* The word penis itself (P-ness, or the quality of P) illustrates this point in a striking way.

---

*The spoke of a wheel is esoterically connected. The Logos, or the Word of God, radiates from the Central Sun to the outer limits of Creation as the spoke of a wheel extends from the hub to the rim. As the spoke of a wheel braces it, so does the speech of man strengthen him. By sounding out his thoughts, man becomes God's "spokesman," His extension.

In this connection consider the word *agape* (from the Greek, meaning God's love for humanity). It can be broken down into ag-ape. In other words, God expresses His love for man by extending Himself (sounding out—Pe), and so through transformation (G) He became man. So great was his love (agape) that He sacrificed his only son; that is, He "extended" himself (made himself visible) for the sake of man.

Other male-aspected P words, projecting from the center, often force-fully (as opposed to the interior, hidden aspect of the female), are *pipe, pep* (energy bursting forth), *potent, peep* (to come into view), *penetrate, pounce, peck, prick, poke, push, pull, put, pat, pomp, pow, pike, pile, putt, puncture, pique, piquant, pooh, pap, pooped** (exhausted, overextended), *pin, pump, pillar, pillage, prey, pickax, pelican, pupa* (from a root meaning "swelled up" or pushed out), *pup* (cone-shaped, a tent), *puppet* (controlled by someone else, thus an extension), *puppy* (full of pep), *pace* (unit of length), *perk, pop* (as verb), *paddle, pendant, power, pale* (pointed stake), *pan* (from an Indo-European root meaning to swell), *para-* (going beyond), *patri* (father), *pitter-patter, piston, pestle, paunch, paw, pee, pitch* (as verb), *pay, peak, peal, pedal, pelt* (as verb), *pen, percuss, perch, phew, phooey* (echoic of the sound of expectoration), *pluck, punch, plus, plume, plumb* (as verb); *poly, pons, poof, pout, probe, pro* (from an Indo-European base meaning forward), *propel, puff, poof!* (bursting away or bursting into view).

---

*\*Poop* is also slang for excrement—poured out or used up. (Cf. *pyo,* a combining form meaning *putrid.)*

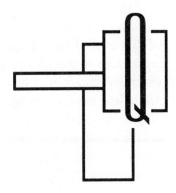

The seventeenth letter of the English alphabet, Q, can be traced back to the Hebrew *Quoph*, (back of the head), or home of the queen of the dark chamber. The darkness of the womb is required for the seed to germinate. Indeed, the root (or *tail*) emerging from the Q symbolizes the potential of growth.

The Q can be likened to the dark side of a mirror, without which reflection (thinking) is impossible because contrast is needed for development. The devil came into his own to challenge the rule of God. The tail on the Q can be likened to the devil's tail, or the incipient self pushing up from the dark interior towards the light of day (cf. *queue* as pigtail).

In English the U is invariably conjoined to the Q to form what can be called the compound letter Qu. Esoterically, this brings out the contrast between the light and the dark, as the U (You) is the world of the other, which confronts us when we emerge from the cave of darkness (Q). It is only in this interface between light and dark that the self (the tail of the Q) develops.

This division is suggestive of the word *quasi* (half). Then there is the sense of *quest* (moving out into the world—from Q to U). *Questions* are asked and *queries* are raised. At the interface there is a *quickening*, with the attendant *quakes, quivering, quarreling, qualms,* and *quips* of life as we follow our intuition (the sparks on the anvil of Q) and move out into the perilous world. *Qabbalah* and *Quran* (spelled alternatively with a K) point to this dark, interior mystery, the mystery of being cut off from the light for the sake of creating a *queen,* or the creative will. In the midst of the nurturing darkness there is a stillness or quiet. Related words are *quit* (to leave off activity) and *quench* (to extinguish). Consider also the words *quell* and *quash*—the basic meaning is "to quiet down."

In *quad* (four) there is an essential Q characteristic, for the four symbolizes the world, which is the womb that sparks intuition. The world is the womb in which the self develops, and so the tail, symbolic of the "clinging" (prehensile) and "curlicued" self!

The word *cue,* a homonym for the letter Q, is a perfect reminder that when one misses a line in life, the Q-faculty from the back of the head can always fill in what was left out. Also, the word *cute* (cu-ku-qu) means, among other things, "clever", "sharp," "shrewd"—a perfect description of the Q's intuitive faculty.

As involved in both *quality* and *quantity* (inner Q and outer U), the QU is expressive of them both.

*Quiddity* and *quite* express the purity of the Q's conceptions—the essential nature of the intuition.

The common Latin words *quis* (who, cf. *quiz*) and *quid* (what) ask questions. The letter Q reminds us that intuition arises out of reflection, or beholding oneself in the mirror of the world. The world compels us to see ourselves, and beholding that image on the screen of manifestation, we wonder who we are, what we are doing here, and where we are going. This process of turning back to the interior (the Q, or the back of the head) generates the questions and the answers.

Assigning the name *quark* to a fundamental building block of matter was a stroke of intuition, for the Q houses that which is basic, fundamental, and essential.

The "mind your P's and Q's" is advice pertaining largely to manners—deporting oneself socially. No one seems to know the origin. Possibly, some say, it served as warning to children who were learning the alphabet. However, it makes good sense esoterically, for it suggests that we consider not only the outward aspect of behavior (the P's, extending themselves), but also the inner aspects (the interior Q, or intuition). It acknowledges the universal truth that we live both an inner and an outer life, both of which should ideally be reflected in our manners.

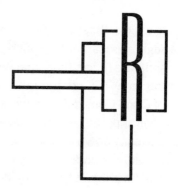

The eighteenth letter of the English alphabet, R, is derived from the He-brew *Resh* (head). The Q, referring to the back of the head, symbolizes the receptive dark faculty of intuition at our creative core, while R designates the entire head and symbolizes the *will,* as in the expression "headstrong." The will is a movement originating from the center of our being and ex-presses our desire to reach out and be "other-than-ourselves." The force of R in the word *radius* illustrates this emanation from the center. So does the word *are.* To say "I am" is to be rooted in the center, the matrix (M) of your being, for out of this center of light the I burns brightly. To say "you are" introduces another dimension of being, for by this declaration "the other" is born. Moving out toward this other to establish an I/Thou rela-tionship involves extending the center (I am) to the circumference (you are). Both are connected by the *radius, ray,* or *R* (are). Clearly there is an iden-tity here: "you are," as circumference, expressing the extent* of my world (my "I am").

This is the essence of R. All the rest is derivative. For instance, *Ra,* the sun god, *radiates* from the central sun. A *roar* expresses that will. To *run* is

---

*Note the word *belong* (meaning *to possess*) as a contraction of two words—*be* and *long.* Thus for something to *belong,* as possession, means simply that it is an extension ("long") of one's being (be-long).

to express that movement physically (cf. *rush, race, rash*). A *rishi* is a Hindu sage, an incarnation of God's will. The word itself is derived from the Sanskrit *rasa* (juice, fluid, that which "overflows" or moves out from the central core). (Cf. *rex* and *rabbi*—expressing the will of the world and the will of God.) Consider also the English words *rise, rose* (moved upward from a central point), *reach, rah-rah* (cheering one on), *ire, rage, radiant, root* (growing down to/from the center), *raid, rail* (to complain against, or, like a radius extending out as tracks), *rake* (derived from *reg*—to stretch out), *real* (moving out from the center; existence as opposed to istence), *ram, ramble, ramp, rampart, roam, range, rip, riot, ravage, rogation* (from "to stretch out the hand," or cf. *interrogate*), *err* (originally to wander off without direction or to stray from the center).

The word *rare* means uncommon, seldom found, tending toward the circumference, stretched out, dispersed. A *rare* steak is lightly cooked, without the intensity of that central fire. *Rear* means in the background, far off. The sound of a *roar* moves out toward the periphery.

*Rude, roast, red,* and rabid expresses the intensity of the R, the force of its will.

*Right, rule, regal, royal, regent, regulate,* and *reckon* are words that derive from the concept of straight, not curved or twisted (to lead, direct, move from one point to another, as a *ray* extends from the center and a *regent* extends his hand to *rule* his people).

In Latin, *res* means *thing,* or that which emerges from the central core.

The prefix *re* means *back, again, anew,* (as in *repay, restore, retell, reappear*). Here the R moves out to the edge and returns again, repeating the cycle and conforming to the universal principle that every letter can become its own opposite. Thus, any radius extended far enough will return to itself—*re!*

Or as coordinating conjunction introduces an alternative (this *or* that), which in its most primordial sense reflects the relationship between center and circumference (to be *or* not to be). The basic alternative *(or)* in life is istence or existence, life or death. The word *or* illustrates this in a near-hieroglyphic way: O represents the center or circle, while R moves away from the center as a radius. The R can be seen as the hieroglyph of a stick-man moving forward (Ɍ).

The sound *or* (aur) also means "radiant light" or "gold," as in *aurum.* In *oral* (cf. *oracle, orison*) there is the reference to speech—that which *radiates* or flows out of the mouth *(orifice)*. In *mem-or-y* we have the light of the sun *(or)* reflected on the waters *(Mem)* of the mind. The image is recorded as in a mirror or on a photographic plate. The basic construction of this word is MR—light (radiance or R) recorded on matter (M).

*More*—the play of light radiating out (R) and reflecting onto the mirror of manifestation (M), which creates the illusion of one sun appearing as an infinite number of suns, reflected in a hall of mirrors or the facets of a diamond.

In *mer* (sea) the waters of manifestation (M) reflect that radiant light (R). In *mere* (as a *mere* child) the indication is undiluted purity. *Mire* is a step further along; the mud of manifestation has sullied the waters (cf. *mar*).

Although the word *awe* is not quite like *or,* still there is the esoteric sense of it, for to stand in *awe* before God is to experience a radiance that inspires fear and wonder.

As suffix, *or* refers to a person or thing *(inventor, actor)* or to a quality or condition *(terror, horror)*. Like the indirect article, which adds grace to every noun (identifying it with the Absolute), the suffix *-or* adds radiance to a concept, so that no matter how far removed it is from the center, it still arises from it and imparts that warmth.

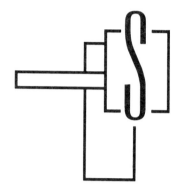

S, the nineteenth letter of the English alphabet, is derived from the Semitic *Shin\* (tooth)*. (The S on its side, in a series, generates an almost hieroglyphic pattern resembling teeth: ∿∿∩.) The key concept here is transmutation, for the tooth is one step in the chain of events that prepares food for digestion and ultimate assimilation. The food is first broken up into pieces[†] and fragmented by chewing. Thus the one becomes many, which is ech-

---

*Some scholars believe that the S is derived from *Samech* (the fifteenth letter of the Hebrew alphabet (prop, pillar, testis, "phallic egg"). The basic sense of Samech is foundation, support, that which sustains. Surely the fertilized ovum (cf. testis as seed-bearer) is the foundation of the man, and a "pillar" props up his "temple". Some believe the *Shin* represents only the SH sound, but this is doubtful, as the *Shin* has been used for the S sound as well. In any case, I regard the SH as virtually a compound letter, for to conjoin S and H is to say, in the language of the Qabbalah, that S transmutes H (or self), reducing it to ashes, which leaves the S standing alone! Actually it is the H that makes the S *shin-e*. Without H there would be no burning bush—no combustion of self. The *Samech* supports the S as infrastructure (cf. the word *sustain*). In its "egg aspect" plurality is generated, and as cosmic egg it is none other that the sun itself (cf. the golden yolk). The *Samech* can also refer to divisions within the circle, or multiplicity (cf. the shin) within the whole or zero presence. Thus *Shin* and *Samech* can be seen as two aspects of one integrative process.
[†]Cf. *se*, as prefix, meaning apart (as in *select*).

68

oed in the role the S plays in the generation of plurals (as in boy to *boys*, cat to *cats*, hat to *hats*). Since the female, as "wombman," is the multiplier of forms, giving birth to our myriad conceptions, the suffix -*ess* (S) signifies the female, as in *lioness, actress, seamstress, poetess*. He is also converted to *she* with the prefix S, and the addition of an S to *Mr.** generates *Mrs.* An unwed female is referred to as *Miss* or *Ms.* (Note also sister.)

The S is also used to create the possessive (the *boy's* hat, the *girl's* coat). This also stems from the concept of transmutation, for to transmute or assimilate something is to make it one's own—to *possess* it. Hence the possessive case. (Note the four S's in *possess!*)

Digestion, the oven of transmutation, can be likened to a burning up process. When cattle are branded, a mark is burned onto them, identifying them as a *possession*.

A key S word is the word *is* itself, meaning *to be*. When something *is*, it exists. This is a curious paradox, because the construction of the word reveals that to be *(is)* connotes burning or transmutation.† So a man who *is* (cf. *esse*—to be) is aflame with his being, living his life in the furnace like the Three Holy Children. Even the sound *is* (*izzzz*) recalls the sound of a burning fuse. Consider, too, the words *essence* (S-sense), that which is left over after the dross is destroyed; *esoteric* (S-oteric), the "inner sense"; and *assess*, the true evaluation or assessment of that which remains after the transmutation.

The word *so*, as an adjective, means "true," "in reality," as in "That is *so!*" In other words, when all the dross has been consumed the bare bones of truth are revealed.

In the word *see*, the S, is the prototypal transmuting agent (the sun), which burns through the husk or covering in order to *see*. A *seer* is someone who has developed this insight and can "see through" things.

To *saw* something with a tool is to burn through it, just as a *sore* is a burning, festering wound (radiating—R—with heat, like a ball of fire, thus SR—*sore*).

The shape of the S is appropriately serpentine, for the serpent, in shedding its skin, also renews itself, as the S does through burning. The serpent

---

*The terminal R in Mr. can be seen as indicating will or strength.
†As does the sun. Compare the cognate *shine* with the transmuting *shin*.

is also a symbol of desire, tempting man to eat of the sacred fruit in the Garden of Eden. In partaking of this fruit, man multiplies, forming the plural of himself like the stars in the sky. He also becomes *possessed* of a self, which is the beginning of individuation. Thus , through desire (*de-sidus* or the light of star) Man consumes himself. He eats (in German, *essen*).

*Is* can be considered in relationship to *am* and *are*. The I as chief reflector ("I think, therefore I am") associates with the M, or sign of reflected life: *I AM. You* (referring to the other) is associated with the R, which like a radius or ray moves to and from the center: *You are. He* becomes *three* and is outside the I/Thou relationship. By the fire of transmutation (isness) I and Thou become *He,* the symbol of the godhead. (Cf. the utterance *soham*—I am He, equivalent to Thou Art That.) Thus, *Is* as Third is the synthesizing force as opposed to I (thesis) and You (anti-thesis.)

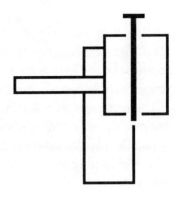

T, the twentieth letter of the English alphabet is derived from the Semitic *Tau*, cross. "Crossing over" forms the very fabric of life itself. Our clothes, for example, by and large consist of thousands of threads that interweave (the warp and woof), forming an impressive array of little crosses. Thus , even to wear clothes* is to bear the weight of the cross or the weight of manifestation. Where the threads intersect, eternity intersects with time. That Christ died on the cross means in this respect that he was renewed[†] at the crossroads. His point of emergence, or transformation, was at the juncture of time and eternity. In his teaching he was able to equate both.

The cross he bore represents the vertical and horizontal stresses which he had to learn to equilibrate. Through crucifixion, Christ died[‡] to himself in time and in so doing realized his eternal nature. Having once effected this, he was no longer identified with either time or eternity. His allegiance was now to God, the Holy Ghost, who can come and go in peace, either as the Father or as the Son.

The T-cross is therefore a point of emergence where time (the horizon-

---

*Cf. tatting—lace made by looping and knotting.
[†]Cf. Tet, the lunar New Year celebrated in parts of Asia.
[‡]This dying is to be taken symbolically only. Dying to the body is rather easy compared with dying to the self.

tal line) is raised up to the level of eternity: the Son of Man *is* the Son of God. Since the equation is solved by the sacrifice of self, the life force can move back and forth from istence (eternity) to existence (time) through the imperceptible eye of a needle.

The word *teat* (also *tit*) illustrates the concept well, for at this juncture the mother and child nourish each other, expressing their mutual love. In the same way does eternity nourish time, and time, eternity.

In Hindu philosophy TAT refers to the Absolute, that which is time/ eternity.

Something that suits someone to a *tee* suits exactly, precisely, referring to that point of crossing over where time is born out of eternity. (Cf. "X marks the spot.") This can also be said of *it* and *at*: *it* refers to a thing fixed in a space and time (that's where *it* is), and *at* means the point or location where a thing is. *It* also refers to the Ultimate, being the mysterious point through which God emerges and renews himself.

In *to*\*there is movement toward an object or destination, the movement of all life toward that point where time meets eternity and they are at one. As an object falls toward the center of the earth, so too does each soul gravitate toward the center of being: the cross, or T. Tote, in its esoteric sense, is to carry one's cross to this point, and *toot* is to sound it out, to strike the note of unity. A tot (cf. *tit*, meaning little, as in *titmouse*, and *tittle*, a small amount) is a newly emerged being who has crossed over from eternity to time. *Total* refers to the All: time + eternity.†

In *taut, tight,* and *tie* there is a binding back to the source. (Cf. the word *religion*, which means to join again). The cross is the tie that makes liberation possible. Something that *teeters* or *totters* is on the verge of changing state, which the T as cross symbolizes. In *tattered* and *tatty*, the worn out rags of the being, identified with time, are renewed at the cross of time and eternity as one receives a garment of light. The Japanese *tea* ceremony is designed to support the meditative mood that creates the conditions for crossing over (T) from one state of consciousness to another.

---

\*In the homonym *two* there is division, or breaking up. The motion can be illustrated with a double arrow: Eternity (←——————→) Time.
†The arithmetical sign for addition is a cross (+) because it represents such a point of growth.

In *tit for tat,* meaning *retaliation,* "tit" connotes little and "tat" big (the Absolute!) The apparent meaning is that equal blows are being exchanged for the garment of light ("TAT," as in TAT TVAM ASI). A *tutor* is a source of learning, as is the cross. *Tut* expresses annoyance (the burden of carrying one's cross), as if someone had crossed you.

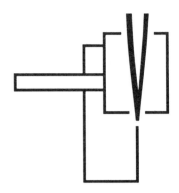

V, the twenty-second letter of the English alphabet is derived (like the F) from the Semitic *Vau* (nail). Historically, U and V were used interchangeably until the U took on its present role as vowel and the V as consonant. An inner relationship still persists, however, as the U, signifying the other, has also imprinted its meaning on the V, which penetrates man's world even to the periphery, the symbolic domain of the devil.*

The V's wedge shape admirably suits it for this symbolic penetration, as in the following words: *invade, invest, vaccinate, vantage, vanguard, very, vanquish, volition, voracious, velocity, dive, vandal, vie, victory, ventilation* (hostile encounter), *velicate* (pluck out) *vampire, vector, verb,* (active element), *venery* (hunt), *vatic* (prophetic, or penetrating the future), *vast, vermi, vortex, vise, divide.*

The V, shaped like an arrowhead, enables man to explore the resources of the universe, the vast emptiness in which he desires to plant the seed of life. The V is not only invasive but also descriptive of the *void,* into which the prodigal son has wandered. Consider the following "empty" words: *vacuum, valley* (dug out), *vacant, vas* (a duct), *vein* (in the sense of hol-

---

*The devil is often depicted as goat-like, with a V-shaped head. He needs this as a "digging tool" to penetrate the outermost reaches, for his esoteric function is to "devil-op" (develop).

lowed-out tube), *vessel, vehicle* (as vessel, conveyor; a vehicle also moves forward or penetrates), *void, vapid, vapor, vanish, vanity* (spiritual emptiness), *vagina, vulva, vague, vagabond* (wandering), *virgin, verge* (on the edge).

The active pursuit of life wherever it can be found (embodied in the concept of the devil as developer) generates hybrid *vigor* (breeding in an alien element), exemplified by the following words (actually a subset of the "penetration" series): *virile, vital, viva, vivacious, vim, vigor, verve, vibrant, volcanic, vivid, valid, value, valor, valiant, vigil, virtue, veracity.*

As can be expected, the opposite is also generated, as the consequences of this penetration into the Void can be *virulent* as well as *invigorating.* (It all depends on the third force—attitude.) Consider the following: *virus, vice, virulent, vile, villain, vulgar, vicious, violate, vitiate, vixen, voodoo.*

Since there is often resistance to this penetration, the polarities being constantly at war with each other, a subset of similar words can be generated: *veer, varus* (abnormally bent or turned), *valgus* (bent or twisted position), *vacillate, vicissitude, vary.*

The *Vedas* are Hindu books of wisdom (V as penetrating insight—cf. the Latin *videre,* to see, and also the English word, *vision*). To make a *vow* is to be joined (cf. the V's hieroglyphic meaning of nail—indeed, the point of a *nail* is V-like) to your creative center, to your God. (It is symbolically a form of moving toward or penetrating.)

*Von,* as in *von* Bismarck, means of ("joined to") the Bismarck family.

*Venus* (the goddess of love) is from the Indo-European *wenos* (desire, to strive for), which is the essence of V. The primal act of disobedience (the eating of the forbidden, sacred fruit) was in truth an act of *love* (or penetration—V—to the eternal sphere—L).

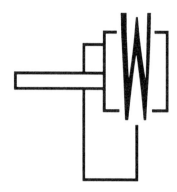

The twenty-third letter of the English alphabet, W, is derived (like U, V, and F) from the Hebrew *Vau* (nail, hook).

As the U implied the not-I, or other, the "double U" (W) implies reciprocity, a reflecting back of identity, the realization that Thou Art That. In water, the universal reflecting medium, the W expresses this concept of identity: to gaze upon one's reflection is to gaze upon one's self-image, the W expressing the mystery of reflected, creative being.

Consider the W words that have to do with reflection (thinking, or asking questions): *what, when, whence, where, whether, which, who, whose, why.*

Other W words can be traced back to the concept of turning, twisting, whirling, or bending, and all originate from the basic idea of bending back on the self to behold the identity of I and Thou as in a mirror: *worm, warp, wrinkle, wobble, wire, weave, worry* (to be twisted inside), *weird, wrestle, wriggle, wring, wrist, wry, wrong* (twisted), *wroth, wince, whorl, whirl, wheel, world, warf* (Indo-European base—to turn), *wear* (as verb, to turn a ship about), *weak* (bending or yielding), *week* (period of change), *whir, wicker, wicket, wicked* (crooked), *wipe* (Indo-European base—turning motion), *wind* (as verb), *withe, wrangle, writhe, wrench, wreath, wrap, worsted, whole* (returned to itself), *wrest, wave, walk* (turn, roll), *wamble, wise* (turn back on, and behold, the Self), *well* (Indo-European base—to turn or roll like a flow of water), *worth* (Indo-European base—to turn), *wife* (from a source meaning "twisted," "turned," "wrapped"; or a hidden or veiled person).

No wonder the exclamation *wow* is the realization that Thou Art That! The Hebrew derivation of W, *Vau* (nail), connotes that which joins; to utter "wow!" is therefore to rejoice that you are joined to That.) (Cf. also *whee!* and *whoopie!*)

To *wonder* is to reflect on the mysterious of seeming separateness: (*W-one-der,* that the W [double-you] is one).

The word *war* is probably derived from the Frankish *werra* (confusion, strife)—confusion and strife over the identity of the enemy. The esoteric key can be found in the word itself, for the initial W indicates that the enemy is none other than "you." The R represents a clash of wills, but surely it is a sciamachy, a shadow play, a suicidal attempt at transcendence, with an alienated double-you (W) slashing at itself. *War* backwards reads *raw,* which in this connection can mean unsophisticated, uncivilized, or primitive, the clash of one blind self against another.

To *worry* is to spin around in circles at the mercy of self, instead of being able to stand outside the self and view the situation objectively. To turn back on the self can be liberating or binding, depending on one's attitude and how one goes about doing it.

In *we* the double-you (W, or I and Thou) is joined, which homonymically reduces itself to *wee.* Through one end of the telescope everything looks large, but seen from the other end it shrinks. It all depends on one's perspective.

In *woo* (to endear) the W as linkage is clearly evident. In *woe* (in a sense, the opposite of *woo*),* the linkage is broken and the double-you is ascendant. It represents our alienation.

In the word *woman* the W as *Vau,* or nail (the ancient meaning of W), indicates woman as a partner joined to man. (Cf. the word *female.* The F

---

*Literally hundreds of examples can be given of the same word (or in this case, a word that sounds like it) engendering its own opposite. For instance, consider the word *cleave,* which means at once "to cut asunder" and "to cling to." And surely the I of man is a grand conception, yet the lower-case "i" (ego) often drags him down. These "identical opposites" are the two hands of man that fashion the world. When understood properly they neutralize each other and liberate us from polarities. This is the peace that surpasses understanding.

is also derived from the Semitic *Vau*—nail—so that female is that which is joined to the male. Wife, too, can be rendered as joined (F) to the W, or "other you.")*

The strength of joining that W lends to a word is evident in the following:

*Wise* (w-is-e): joined (W) to being (is).

*Wit* (in its most general sense, the mind): that which is joined (W) to IT (the universal Self): w-it.

*Well* (in the most general sense of whole, healthy, flowing): that which is joined (W) to El or God w-ell.

*Whole* (W-hole): that which is joined (W) to Nothing (hole) (i.e. "all").

*Will:* that which is joined to the highest principle (il-el-al-allah) develops will.

*Wall:* that which seemingly divides is a mirror image (double-you) of the all.

*Win:* to conquer Nothing (or to be joined—W—to Nothing), for N in this connection means the spirit of No-Thing. This is the ultimate winning or victory. The word *Venus* (love) is connected to *win,* as is *ween* (to think), for to think is to desire to know, to be in love with life; responding in kind, life reveals itself to the thinker as a lover reveals herself to her beloved. In this sense there is a victory; something is *won* (cf. *one* or unity), but it cannot be clutched at, for there is no-thing there!

*Way:* the Tao, or path of life—a critically important word, esoterically meaning joined (W) to A (the First Principle). That is the only path for a human being to walk on. At once it is the lightest (the First Principle being Nothing) and the heaviest, as in *weigh* (cf. *way*) or *weight*.

*World* (cf. *whirl-d*): here the W makes the complete circuit from I to Thou and back again, thereby creating a world that encompasses all beings. The word world itself can be broken down into its components: W-OR-L-D: the light (OR) of heaven (L) joined (W) to the earth (D). (Cf. *wield,* essentially meaning strength.)

---

*Also, cf. *wife* to *whiff (wif)*: faint smell, hint of what it is like to be whole again and joined to the female principle, to savor the sacred ground of your being.

*Wheel:* essentially, that which moves with and is joined to (W), the Higher Principle (EL). To put it somewhat differently, the two ends (W) meet as one (EL).

*Wake:* to be fully aware is to be *awake.* In the alphabetic analysis wake means to be joined (W) to the K, that is, to that which is most concrete in Man—his core.*

The other side of W is alienation, or one you split off from another, a double-you with no connection. This separation, the other end of W's spectrum, is reflected in the following words: *woozy, worse, wretch, weird, weep, wan, weary, wander, wane, want, war, wound, wacky, wobble, wail, wamble, wanton.* Again, a word of caution: for a staid man to act *wacky* in a purposeful way is eminently sane, and for a Puritan to become *wanton* in a harmless moment of abandon may be just the thing needed to save his soul. The only sane way to walk in this world is on the razor's edge, where the three paths (trivium) meet!†

It is appropriate here to consider the word *write.* In English, the flow of words is from left to right. Hebrew reads from right to left. In the Far East the flow is sometimes vertical. One ancient form of writing, *boustrophedon* (as the ox moves the cart), even flows first one way and then back the other. The English word write has a connotation of the I/Thou relationship built into it with the initial double-you (W). Writing esoterically is of the heart and should flow outward, but the feedback of the world closes the circuit so the heart is refreshed and renewed. The flow from left to right balances the flow from right to left. The addition of Oriental languages that flow vertically makes it possible to see that all the world's languages present themselves together in the form of a cross, at the center of which the Word is revealed.

---

*Yet, WK also generates *weak,* in some respects the opposite of *wake.* It cannot be repeated too often that the letters radiate in many directions. Thus K can be of inestimable value in the *kaaba* but snuff out a life in *kill* or suffocate someone in *choke.* The alphabet mirrors Man, and Man cannot be pigeonholed.
† Strange how this magnificent symbol of the majestic three—the place where three roads meet—has degenerated to trivia—unimportant, meaningless!

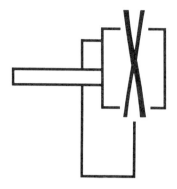

X, the twenty-fourth letter of the English alphabet, is the king of fools among the consonants, succeeding in making itself relatively useless, as the sounds of KS (*axe*) or Z (*xeno*) can readily substitute for it. Yet, in making itself largely superfluous, it is free to take on another role, That role, as fool (meaning "filled with the Spirit" like a *joker*—one who is *joined* or *yoked* to the Spirit) enables the X to stand as a wild card for any other letter. X can equal any quantity in an equation, and when the equation is solved (balanced), X the unknown reveals itself. So with a balanced man: when the equation of his life is solved, the unknown reveals itself through him. He becomes It. "X marks the spot" at the center of the Cross, mysterious point in the linkage between nothingness and being, or istence and existence. From that point all manifested life emerges. No wonder X is also used as the symbol for multiplication.

In Roman numerals, X stands for ten, a perfect number, composed of nothing (0) and something (1) and moving in and out of manifestation, disappearing and reappearing in its own mysterious way. When laid horizontally ($\times$) the X becomes one thousand, for the fool (Christ) is increased (cubed) by surrendering, by being crucified or brought down. Then, when raised up again (resurrected), only heaven is his limit, and he becomes *ten thousand* ($\bar{X}$ = 10,000, where the horizontal bar over the X symbolizes heaven). The bar can also mean minus, that is, the X has been reduced to ashes—to nothing—and as such can enter actively into all things, filling them with the Spirit.

On the X or Cross Christ learned the secret of time and eternity, of life and death, of renewal, and of balancing involutionary and evolutionary thrusts.* The X stands by itself, being at once in the alphabet and outside it. Hence the meaning of the prefix *ex: without, away from, outside of,* as in *expel.†*

The X can have a hard sound as in axe or a soft sound as in Xanadu, for it runs the gamut (like the Fool or Joker) from A to Z, being everywhere and yet nowhere. In sharing the sound of KS it penetrates to the core of material existence, and in masquerading as the Z it soars to the zenith of poetic fancy.‡

---

*Consider the construction of the X itself—two V's reflecting each other, a thrust downward and a thrust upward, which meet at the growing point.

†Consider the prefix *xeno-* (foreign, strange, extraneous) and how well it defines the X. Also, the prefix *xero-* (dry—as in *xerography*). *Dry* is an ancient symbol for dead—dried, mummified. The X, as the unknown nothing, is "dead" (to our senses), but nevertheless the ground of all life. Paradoxically, the prefix *xylo-* means *wood* (as in *xylem*). Thus the X is also that living substance, The Tree of Life, the Cross on which Christ died.

‡The letter X probably originates from the Semitic *Samekh,* meaning "prop," or possibly "fish". But the common denominator is that which supports, as the Fish (the eyes of the sea) is the symbol of the Universal Spirit. The cross that supported Christ—*propped* him up, as it were—was that great unknown X of which man is the embodiment.

The Y, or twenty-fifth letter of the English alphabet, like the F, U, V, and W, can be traced back the Hebrew *Vau* (nail, hook). One may ask why the *Vau* is basic to so many letters. The answer is that the concept of joining (which the nail symbolizes) is essential to life on earth. Indeed, the word *yoga* means "to join," and the word *joy* is an altered form of *join*.* That is, the greatest joy that we can experience is to join with our Creative Principle. Even the word *religion* means "to tie back" (re-ligio), to join with God.

Expressing this coupling force (cf. *yin, yoke*), the Y is a thinly disguised hieroglyph of Christ on the cross ( ) or a being with outstretched arms rejoicing and affirming life.

Enclosed in a circle ( ), the Y presents three radii, symbolic of the mystery of God the Father, God the Son, and God the Holy Ghost. The letter Y confronts us with the fundamental question, "Why?" that every thinker, sage, and hero has wrestled with. The question is a koan and cannot be answered in linear language, and so the Y does not answer but affirms—expresses life fully (cf. yes!). The sphinx poses the riddle but it is for us to respond by becoming *that which is asked—the unfoldment of the three.* (Recall the riddle: What walks on four feet in the morning, two in the afternoon, and three in the evening? It is man, for as an infant he crawls on

---

*Esoteric only—not etymological.

82

all fours, as a youth he walks erect, and as an elder he is assisted by a cane—his "third foot"—which is actually a symbol for something much more profound. As an elder the man may come to understand the Y (why) of his existence—his three emanations, or the Law of Three.)

As emanation from the center the Y is a measure of manifestation, as in *year, yuga,* and *yester* (as in *yesterday*). It is also a measure of activity, affirmation, intensity, as in *yes, aye, yang, yearn, yammer, yagger, Yahweh* (the Creative Principle), *yap, yak, yock, yare* (brief, active quick), *yatter* (continuous chatter), *yacht* (originally, a pursuit ship), *yoga, yank* (sudden, strong pull), *yawn* (recharging the fatigued battery), *yawp, you* (cf. I am/ you are, where the *you* is the extension from the center, the affirmation of its creative essence), *ye, yea, yeah, yean* (to bring forth a lamb), *yeast* (rising), *yield, yell, yellow* (gleaming, radiating), *yelp, yen* (strong longing), *yenta* (Yiddish for gossipy woman), *yep, yip, yipe, yippee, yod* (the hand that reaches out and grasps), *yodel, yonder* (forward in space), *yore* (backward in space), *yoo-hoo, young* (freshly emerged), *yo-yo, yuk, yowl, yummy.*

In the word *you* (as in U) the Y brings into play the son or ray (radius, in manifestation as other (God the Son in contrast to God the Father). But as all three aspects are combined in the Y (positive, negative, neutral), the negative, passive principle is also introduced in the significant word *yin*—the principle that complements the *yes* with its own inevitable *no*. Between these two forces Christ is crucified. As the third principle (the Y) he is the anointed one.

As suffix the Y can denote "action of," as in *inquiry, entreaty and sophistry,* expressing the Y's intensity and radiant activity. As suffix it also indicates quality, condition, or "characterized by," as in *jeopardy, happy, healthy, honesty.* When we are *happy* we radiate, express, or assert that condition. Happiness emanates from us as a radius emanates from the center of a circle. It characterizes us.

As the mathematical ordinate, Y (as opposed to the abscissa, which is designated by X) is a vertical axis that symbolically rises out of the ground moving toward the sun in affirmation.

The Y is also the sixth vowel and can substitute for (and sound like) an I or an E, as in *Bobby* and *yclept*). It can play the role of vowel or consonant (soul or body) because its nature, being *three,* partakes of both. In a sense it can be compared with the X, the extraneous consonant, because it imitates already existing sounds. To that extent the Y is also superfluous, for as vowel it imitates other sounds (in *myrrh* it even imitates a U). But its presence is important, for as the sixth vowel it can be transformed into at least three others (I, E, and U). It can do this (cf. the X as the unknown) only because it is not identified with itself as Y. Like the queen in chess, the Y and the X can move in any direction across the board.

As a vowel it represents one of the six lights that illuminate the Word. Just as man has five senses (and a sixth intuitive or spiritual sense), so too with the vowels. And just as the sense of touch can be seen as more basic than sight, hearing, tasting, and smelling, which are but special modifications of it (e.g., light touches the mechanism of the eye, a sound touches the ear), the six vowels all arise from the Grand Aleph or Sacrificial A.

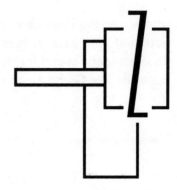

The Z is derived from the Hebrew *Zayin* (arrow). It is voiced like the sound of a weapon cleaving the air. Thus we have the onomatopoetic *zing, zip, zap, zoom, zounds* ("God's wounds," or the piercing power of Z), and the words *zest, zeal, zenith, zen, zany, zowie, Zeus* (the supreme deity), *zombie* (supernatural power), *zillion, zonk, Zohar* (brightness), *ziggurat, Zion* (from a word meaning hill), *zaftig* (sending one off, "soaring")—all echoing the force behind the arrow.

In the prefix *zoo-* there is the quickening, animating force (cf. *zaftig*). *Zero*, symbol of the Absolute, is at once the highest and the lowest, containing within itself all numbers. *Zone* (from gird, belt) and *zodiac* (circle) reflect the all-encompassing force of Z, for as weapon it returns symbolically to the one who wields it.

The Z is closely related to the S (cf. *surprise, surprize*), for the tooth is an archetypal weapon. Thus both the S and the Z cleave the one into the many, thereby creating a powerful activating force. *Za-* used as an intensive prefix (as in the words *zalophus* and *zapus*) has the basic sense of *very*, reflecting the force of the arrow or the strength of the sword.

It is appropriate that the last letter of the alphabet symbolizes power actualized, whereas the first letter symbolizes potential power. The last letter is also the least used. That is to say, man has not actualized his full potential, the zero presence still sleeping within him—note the onomatopoetic sound for sleep: zzzzzzzz—for the seed of the A is still scattered. The Grand Aleph or actualized A is yet to be born.*

---

*The Z as that actualized power can be seen as an aspect of N (lay it down on its side and it becomes a Z), which is the power of the Spirit or the power of Nothing (cf. "none" to "zero").

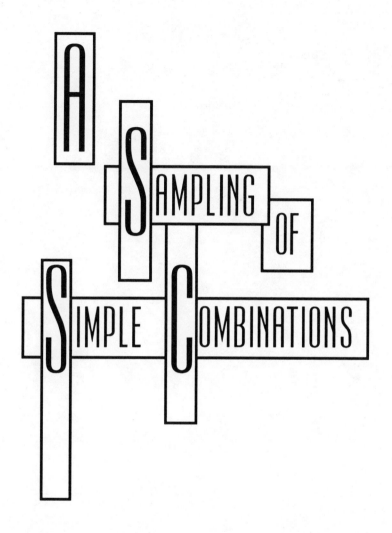

A Sampling of Simple Combinations

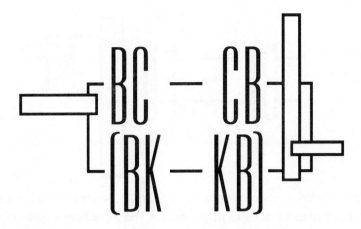

B and K together enclose (B), and compress (K), as in *bake.* A *bike* is a nest of wild bees or wasps—that is, an enclosed, compressed force. The *beak* of a bird is a compacted substance. The male among deer, antelope, goats, and rabbits is the *buck,* probably because the male is characterized by strength or "horniness." In the phrase "buck up," meaning to *brace one-self,* the same idea is evident. The *back* is the source of strength, the foundation that supports us (Atlas carried the world on his *back*). To *rebuke* is to reprimand sharply, in a forceful, compact manner. A *book* contains (it is hoped) the concentrated thoughts of the author, "baked over" as it were by the mind. A *cab* is a hollowed out (K as mold) enclosure (B). A *cob,* generally, is a rounded lump. The *Kaaba* is a black stone (concentrated essence) in which Allah's light sleeps. A *cub,* in this connotation, is a concentrated furry mass—the kernel of life (cf. the kernel on a corn *cob*). A *beck* is a small stream, generally with a rocky bottom. The combination appears also in *buccan,* a wooden frame for drying meat; *boccie,* Italian lawn bowls; *bock* (from Hindi *bok*—he-goat), leather made from sheepskin sometimes used in bookbinding; and *buccal,* pertaining to the mouth, especially as the organ of chewing.

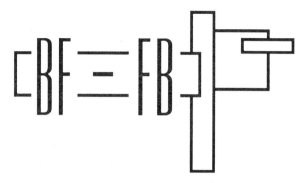

The B as circumscriber makes a home for man, while the F is the force or power joined to it that lights up the house. The word *beef* is generated, the meat or flesh of man that houses the Spirit.* FB yields *fabric*,† that which covers man and shelters him. Related, in an inner sense, is the word *fable* (imaginary, fictitious), the web of Maya that is spun because of the circumscription of the Spirit. The word *fib* designates a lie, or falsification ("made of whole cloth" or fabric) because once we are covered by Being (B or Beth, house) our vision becomes veiled and we are subject to deceit (cf. the Biblical story of Jacob's deception of Isaac, whose eyes were dim with age). This house (shell) that we live in serves as *buffer* (BF) against the blows or *buffets* (cf. *biff*) of fate.‡

A colorful word generated from this forceful impact of Spirit against itself is *buffoon* (etymologically, from "a puff of wind"; cf. *Fool,* from *follis,*

---

*The now obsolete words *fub* and *fubby* (fat, chubby) are an echo of the beef (or swelling) that renders the Spirit visible when it comes into B-ing. To be fat with life is to *be* with it.

†Man is a *fabricator* or weaver of cloth (the vehicle of the Spirit, or Mercavah), which is his own "cocoon". Thus he fabricates or tells lies and is deceitful, because his light is concealed (cf. *fob* and the obsolete *fub*—to trick, deceive).

‡A *buffer* protects against the *buffets* or blows of Fate. In other words, once Man has evolved a shell, forces like those locked up inside him "bang on his gates," buffeting him because of his own self-imposed resistance. Whereas before there was Nothing (istence), now there is a division, and the two cymbals clash to produce the sound of unity. Instinctively they buffet only because they have this deeply rooted urge to join together again, to merge as one organism (cf. *faber,* worker, "he who puts together").

a bag of wind). That is, we are beings who can laugh* at and with the buffeting of Fate because we have learned to roll with the punches. We laugh because we realize that the so-called adversity actually tests our mettle.

*Feeble* (FB) and *baffle* (BF) characterize the state of confusion created by this *fabrication,* for the more likely response to this buffeting of the Spirit (veiling its Light) is confusion. Maya requires the wisdom of a fool or buffoon to see through it. The friction generated by this opposition generates life, or heat† (cf. *febrile).*

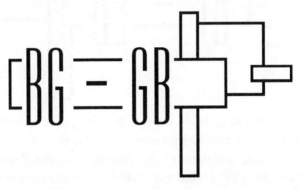

B is an activity that encloses, sets off, and limits; G is a movement toward transformation. When affixed to each other they generate the idea of a swelling, which conceals an inner space. In *beg* there is a need to be filled or swelled. *Big* is swelled out, near to bursting, as in a full gut. *Bag* is a hollow enclosure, like a womb. A *bug* is usually baglike in shape—*bulging* (cf. "bug-eyed"). A *bug* is also a defect or an impediment, based on the concept of interrupted flow that builds up to a swelling. Vanity *bogs* down the life force until it is near to bursting. The *bogyman* frightens children because the waters of life are dammed up in him until he is disfigured (swelled up). A *bog* is spongy ground, swollen with water. *Gab* is idle chatter that fills the air—swells it—with nonsense and thus makes a windbag of the speaker (cf. *fool,* derived from *follis*—windbag.) *Gob* is a lump,

---

*Cf. *boff,* a hearty laugh—the "roar" of the clashing opposites.
†A sick person may have a temperature—a *fever.* How interesting that the opposition of life to itself creates time, temperature, and heat, as well as tempo, the beating of the heart which is the buffeting of fate (for it is certain to kill you!).

(as in *gobble,* to seize greedily and swell oneself with food; also, *goblin,* a misshapen evil spirit. The word *gib* is derived from the Middle English word *gibbe,* a swelling. *Gibbous* means rounded and bulging. *Geb* mean *born* (a budding process, a swelling).

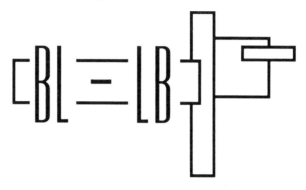

In this combination the key word is *Bel,* the god of heaven and earth (cf. *Baal, Belial*). El is the elevated one: God, who always comes back to himself (L, as rolling) and returns to the source. To prefix El with a B (self-limiting enclosure) defines God as that spirit (El) enclosed in manifestation (B). The word *belle* (beautiful) indicates a spirit encased in form, and earthlocked god. This enclosing of the spirit (limiting the limitless) also generates *ball* (world) (cf. the humorous designation *belly,* swollen ball; in addition consider the following: *bulb, bubble, boil* (swollen), *bill,* and *bull,* the latter two originally derived from *bubble,* that which is blown out but is also concealed). Then there are the words *babble,* a *bubbling* sound; *bleb,* a *blister; blow; bole,* from an Indo-European base "to swell up"; *bale.*

A *bill* or written document is inscribed or sealed (cf. "concealed") within an enclosure, as in *Bible:* the Lord's word, L, inscribed, B. (cf. *bull*—an official document). In *bell* there is a "voiced" document—the sound to unity. (In order for sound to be expressed at all it needs to resonate within a form.)

In the word *Babel,* the imprisoned god (earthbound man), in confusion, attempts to return to the source by an act of accretion (building a high tower), not realizing that in order to accomplish this task the *bubble* (*Babel*) has to burst and be as nothing (the sacrifice of Christ).

Both *lob* and *lobe* (simple expressions of LB) are derived from words that mean hanging or heavy, which can be considered the correlatives of *Bel* (the imprisoned god) and *bale* (evil). Yet LB is also the root of *liberty* (cf. *liebe*—love), for freedom, paradoxically, is born of limitation—that which has fallen.

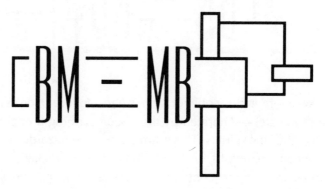

The B initiates activity (to be), and contains it within a boundary (*Beth*, house). The water of manifestation (M) pressing against this enclosure generates an explosive force, as in *bomb, bombast, boom, bump, beam* (radiance); *bumper* (unusually large—a bumper crop); *bumptious* (conceited); *bema* (in the Eastern Orthodox Church the enclosed area surrounding the altar, or place of power, where the sacrifice is made); *bambino* (a child containing all the potential power of the man that will one day burst into bloom; in the word *bum* this power is wasted, deflected, leaking out on all sides; but in *bum* as buttocks (foundation) it is the instinctive source of strength. (Recall the "ass" as burden bearer.)*

In *mob* (MB) there is the potential bursting power of a moving crowd. (Cf. *mobile*—the power of motion from Brownian to cyclonic.) And good Queen *Mab* governs our dreams, wherein lies the potential power of all manifestation. In *mab* (slattern—now obsolete), as in *bum,* the power is wasted, deflected.

---

*To make an ass of oneself is to "expose" your ass, which is to uncover the source of power, the power to "let go"—"excrete," divest the "self." This is considered embarrassing (em-bare-ass) because we become the clothes. The clothes *are* the man, and to be naked is to be like nothing.

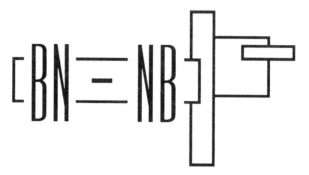

The key word in this configuration is *ban*—to forbid, prohibit, cut off (ex-communicate)—generated by the circumscribing B enclosing and thus "cutting off" the spirit N. This cosmic process is hazardous. The cutting off can become *baneful* if the circulation is unduly blocked. Circumscription is also evident in *bin* (container), *bun* (swelling), and *ben* (son of, a swelling or offshoot). If something has *been,* it is over with, completed, contained. *Bone* is an excellent symbol of this circumscribing process, where the B, as cover, condenses or crystallizes around the "one" (the essence or marrow), and so *b-one* is laid down. When understood qabbalistically, *bane* is transformed into *boon* (cf. *bon*).

The words *nib, nab, nob, nub,* and *neb* all pertain in some way to ideas involving a projecting part (*nab*), point (*nib*), head (*nob*—cf. *knob*), beak (*neb*), protuberance (*nub*). The wayward spirit (N), footloose and fancy free, is forced to come to a head, which brings it to a point of concentration. Thus projected, it can be *nabbed*—snatched, cut off.

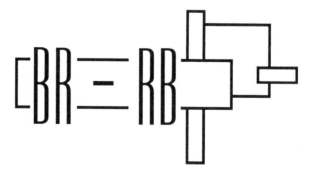

B, as the foundation or the beginning, forms the base against which the R, or the force of will, struggles (cf. *bray*—to pound into a powder). Thus the exclamation *Brrrr!* (it's cold!) generates its own heat. So to say *Brrr!* is an instinctive attempt to kindle a flame. (Compare the R as "firestick," rubbing against the B as peat or base.) Thus, once the B sets limits, the R (will) opposes it with intense passion, and desire—fire! Consider in this connection, the RB words *ruby* (its fiery color), *rabbi* (holy fire—cf. *rabid*), *rub* (the heat of friction), *brew* (to steep, boil), *brio* (vivacity, zest, animation).

This willful movement against the base will not only *burn* (BR) but also *bore* a hole (cf. *bury*), which will *bare* the essential element. To *bar*—based on the same principle of friction against a base—is to restrict movement of. Thus it is also the word for the law (the *bar*), which regulates, restricts, confines. A *burden* restricts movement, and to *bear* is to sustain a weight (cf. *bier,* for a coffin, and *burro,* a beast of burden).

Since the R echoes the will and B reflects the activity of making (enclosing), the word *rob,* in this connection, means to appropriate (rope off), or to will as one's own.* The word *robe* is also related, as the robe delineates the owner, and may even stand for him (the robe of office). The word *rib,* as noun, is an arched, enclosing support—the bony robe.†

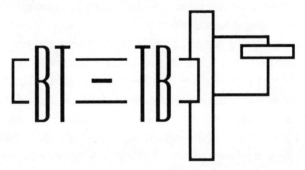

Both T (crossroads to manifestation) and B (the initiation of activity, that which begins or creates) are related concepts and thus reinforce each other.

The word *bit* (a small quantity) illustrates well the concept of life emerg-

---

*Cf. this to the "burning" words—*brrrr!, burn, bore, bare, bar*—for heat as fusing agent is also related to "making one's own", as in *branding* (another BR root).

†*Rib* is probably related to *rive* (to tear apart—cf. Eve as Adam's rib, torn out of, or *derived* from, his inside). She is "split off" from him, created by the heat of friction (RB—rib—cf. to "rib" someone, to tease or make fun of, which arouses anger and wrath. Standing outside of him, Eve now becomes his rival in the sense that she opposes (ribs) him. Woman is man's will or volitive faculty, and as such is essential

ing. It suggests a budding or swelling at the joint at the point where time and eternity meet. This conjoining of the B and T also generates *tube,*\* the hollow (cf. *tibia,*—a hollow bone, and *tub*) or passageway responsible for channeling the life force. (The B itself can be considered a tube. As such it is the first organ of manifestation, a cosmic gut.)

The preposition *but,* in its denotation "except "(all *but* him), expresses succinctly the limits imposed by B (reinforced by T) in its role as circumscriber, for it draws the line or magic circle within which the activity of excepting takes place. This excluding or cutting off is the means by which being emerges out of non-being. *But* for that there'd be no exception—nothing could be differentiated. *Beta,* (the second letter of the Greek alphabet) illustrates the archetypal duality, being and non-being. (Cf. the word *both* and the Hebrew *beth.*)

The word *boat,* as a simple BT word, can be seen in this context as a vehicle (cf. Noah's Ark, the "first " boat) or *mercavah,* which is the form the spirit takes in order to manifest. In this sense a boat is nothing more than a floating tube that rides over the waters of manifestation. (Cf. *boot,* which covers and protects the foot.)

*Bite,* as a quantity cut off, admirably describes the BT process as the universal serpent in a self-enclosed circle consuming itself. It is this bite into the whole that energizes life (the B as vital activity) and makes it possible to digest the experience of existence. Once it bends back on itself, the alpha and omega of the two ends meet, electricity is generated and life begins. It is a self-eating (biting) phenomenon. (Cf. *bait* † food set out as a lure, arousing the desire to bite.) To *beat* is to move or sound rhythmically (as in the heart*beat*) or to mark time. In crossing over from non-being to being the first heartbeat is sounded. *Time begins.*

---

for the individuation process. Eve creates the desire in Adam to claim the world *as his own* (at once the source of his genius, but also the source of his problems!). In literature, sacred and profane, she is also blamed (cf. Eve and Helen of Troy) for man's Fall. But this is only a symbol of a metaphysical process, for without experiencing this Fall, man would never inherit the robe of the gods!

\*Cf. *tube* as tu-be (to be). That is, without that enclosure, existence is not possible.
†*The desire to be* (TB-BT) is apparently the root of all desire, and life first satisfied this desire by consuming *Itself!* The word *cannibal* can be rendered (qabbalistically,

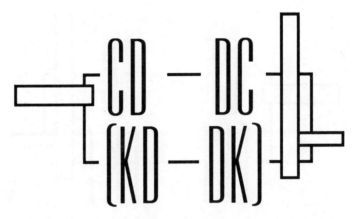

*Code* (principles, rules of conduct, or the restrictions of form) is a key word in this configuration, reflecting the molding (K) character of material life (D). This code is engraved in the fissures of our brain and molded or hollowed out in our hearts.

Many other DK-KD words denote "hollow": *doke,* a hollow depression; *dock,* a hollow in which a ship can be received; *dike,* a ditch or watercourse; *duck,* to go under or hide in a hollow; *deck,* which covers a ship's hold or hollow; *duke* (cf. *ducere*), from to drag or tow, a leader or "channelizer" of men. A *cade* is a barrel; a *caddy* is a small container; a *cod* is a bag; a *cuddy* is a small room, a *kid* is a wooden tub. (*Kid,* referring to the young of several species, may well mean in this connection the product of a mold or womb.) To *cuddle* is to press together, and a *cud* is something to chew over. A *cad* (referring to someone who displays ungentlemanly behavior) is fallen man himself, for the KD in the broadest metaphysical sense refers to the hollowed out space man has implanted himself in. (Cf. Adam *Kadmon,* the archetypal man, the man who fell from heaven, dug himself into the earth, and made for himself a hollow.)

---

but not etymologically), "Cain Abel." Cain, a tiller of the ground, slays his brother, Abel, and plants him (the voice of your brother's blood crieth out to me from the ground) in order to eat him. This is a mythological description of the BT process.

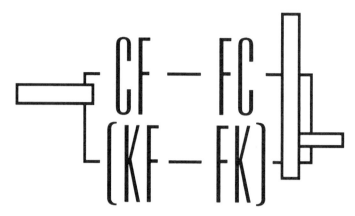

The key to this configuration is the Hebrew letter *Kaf* \* (the English K), indicating that which can be hollowed out, made, or molded. Thus the Latin *facere* (FC), to do or make, and so *fact* and all the other FC words: *fecundate,* make fertile—cf. *fuck; feculence,* making waste; *fictile,* that which can be molded; *fiction,* imaginary happenings; *fake,* make something seem real; *focus,* bring together or make clear.

What is made becomes the *fabric* of our existence and serves as cover or enclosure.† Cf. *caftan* or *Kaph-tan* with the letter *Kaph; coffin; coif; kaffiyeh,* headdress; *fake,* a nautical term for a loop of coiled rope which wraps around itself; *cuff,* originally a glove, now a folding over; *coffer; fyke* (FK), a long bag-shaped net.

Once something is made or formed, maya comes into play, and so *kef* (from the Arabic *kaif,* well-being) is a dreamy condition brought on by narcotics. Also, consider *fike* (original sense, to desire eagerly), to move about restlessly, worry, or fidget. *Fiko* is a worthless trifle, and to be *fickle* is to act capriciously. *Fakir* is an interesting construction. The word is descriptive of an ascetic who makes an intense effort to overcome maya (mold nature, K, make Nature obey, FC, by an effort of will, R).

---

\*The K carries the weight, while the F energizes it.

†The original "fig leaf" covering of Adam and Eve is a curious usage, for the English word, *fig* is related to the Vulgar Latin *fica* and the Latin *ficus*—FC—or the archetypal fabric: that which is made.

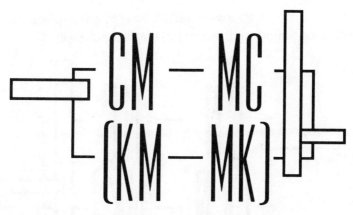

The M and K together represent esoterically, in the broadest sense, frozen matter that has been crystallized or condensed. *Come, coma,* and *comma* are related symbolically to this slowed-down motion or cessation of activity characteristic of this crystalline state. In *coma* there is a cessation of consciousness, in *comma* there is a pause, in *come* there is arrival or a cessation of action (He has *come*\* home.) Also, as an imperative it can mean "See here!" (Stop! Come now!).

*Muck* (MC) is goo or gush (slowed-down matter), and *make* (cf. *made*) is the slowing down of energies or a crystallization. (Cf. Mac—son of—which is also related to make: MacPherson, the son of Pherson, or that which he did make). *Mica* is a crystallized silicate. *Meek,* in one denotation, means deficient in spirit. To *mock,* in one sense, is to disappoint the hopes of; in another, to defy and make futile. Another meaning of mock as a noun is root or tree stump—that which is firmly attached. *Micro* and *macro* (small and large) describe different classifications of matter that has been slowed down, crystallized, or made.

*Kama* is one name for the god of love. Love is at-one-ment, that which has come home or arrived at the still center. It is in one sense the peace that surpasses understanding. The Shinto word *kami* (divine power attributed to supernatural beings) has a similar connotation: that which has arrived, the achievement of the omega point. The MC-CM and MK-KM combinations can reflect the highest (Kama) and the lowest (make, muck) as two ends of the spectrum. *Com,* as a prefix, means with, together (*com-*

---

\*Cf. *calm* (essentially CM with a silent l)—quiet, not agitated.

*pare, compact, compress, compound*). To be with is to be pressed together, compacted, or compressed: matter (M) that is molded (K).

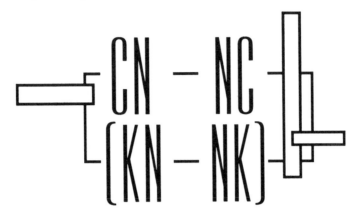

*Keen* and *ken* are words in this configuration (cf. *cunning, canny*). The spirit (N) is sharpened by molding and compressing (K) and brought to a point of concentration or focus (cf. *know*).* By opposing the Spirit (N) and creating resistance (K), man learns how to do. He *can* (CN). This becomes the source of his power (cf. *khan, king, kohen*—priest). *Cain* is the compressed one who slew his brother Abel (mist or spirit)—he ruled over and dominated him and contained his essence.

In *kinfolk* (relatives, family) the concept of a spiritual unit is brought into play, a spiritual affinity (N) that draws together (K). *Kin,* as a suffix, means "little" (the K as compressor), as in *lambkin.* A *koan* (KN) confronts the mind with an impossible situation (e.g., the sound of one hand clapping), the contemplation of which explodes the confined self (K) revealing the original face (N). This is the essence of KN—the *cosmic knower.* For how is it possible for that which is limitless and eternal (N) to become limited and time-bound (K)? *Con,* meaning *against* (pro and *con*), derives from the resistance and the restraint of K. As prefix it means with, together (cf. *confidence*); that is, compressed (cf. *com*). Likewise, NC-NK indicates a nar-

---

*Know, or k-no-w. The kernel of know is a denial—no; that is, knowing is dependent on a narrowing down or focusing of consciousness, a saying of "no" to the All. It's an individuating process, a concentration of attention. Negating goes against the grain and breaks taboos, creating friction and thus light (knowledge).

rowing (the N moving toward nothing, the K reducing or pressing together). Consider the words *neck, nick* (a slit), *nook, knack* (a sharp, compressed sound or skill; cf. *knock*). Also, consider *cane* (a narrow stem), *cuneiform* (wedge-shaped), *cone* and *cant* (in one denotation, the outside angle or corner of a building). In *naked* (NK) the N narrows down to nothing (no "clothes"), the K reinforcing this concept of reduction.* In *nuclear* we are reduced to the most essential element, the kernel (cf. *nux*—nuks-NK—*nut*). *Nickel* is a hard, metallic element.

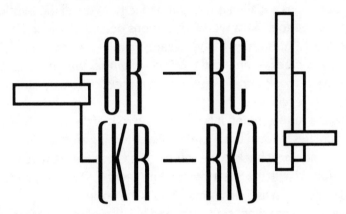

*Core*† is a key word in this configuration. The R, representing fire (will), burns brightly in the midst of the hollow (K, or hard C). Thus, *courage* (CR), *Kyrios* (KR—Lord—seat of power), *cross* (the junction of power where the flame burns at the center), *Roc* or *Rukh* (the Parahamsa, or Great Bird), *rock* (the core of which is that central fire), *Christ* (CR)—the will or intensity of Christ that burns within his being, *corpus, corporeal* (the hollow of the body within which burns the will), and *caro* (flesh—as in *carrion*—that which decays or burns up; also *caries*—decay—and *cremate*). A *car* is the vehicle or "flesh"—shell—of the man.

*Create* (CR) is related to *core* (the seed pocket). Closely related to the concept of creation (from the Indo-European *kre,* to grow) is the word *cry:*

---

*Cf. *nix* (niks—NK) meaning no, *necro* (dead), *nox* (night, dark impenetrable).
†Cf. the Japanese word *kara* (empty)—the power of the core is its emptiness. *Kiri,* in Japanese, means "to cut" (as in *harakiri,* to cut open the belly or the center), pierce the veil, penetrate to the center, or core of emptiness.

a loud sound (as in cry out for help). It is the intensity of the will (R) sounding, resonating, within its own hollow (K). This process echoes the Logos or primordial word that precipitates the cycle of creation (cf. *Cronus*—CR—time). Essentially, this primal word is the creative utterance, like the *cry* "Let there be Light!" But once man becomes trapped in this enclosure, he sheds tears of sorrow, and the cry that he utters now is an instinctive attempt to dissolve and wash away the crystallizations formed by the stopping up of the creative process. As the potter well knows, the pot (K, molding process) does not always turn out perfectly. With all the twisting and turning needed to make a world, distortions occur. Consider the following *Kre* words, illustrative of the hazards involved in creation (CR-KR): *crazy, cruel, crack, cram, crass, crime, crimp, cramp, crunch, cringe, crinkle, crone, crook, cripple, crap, crutch, wreck (RK), crush, carnage, carp (as verb), curse, crick.*

A *crisis* is a turning point. It is the esoteric root of the word *Christ,* a being who creates his own *crisis* for the sake or turning around his evolutionary thrust, moving it back to the source. The CR as the creative fire of the will, conjoined with the S as a transmuting agent (CRS, *crisis*), esoterically spells out the Christ as Transformer. This is the positive aspect of KRE-ing, the crunching, crowding, cramping, and twisting of the soul that enables it to find a new direction or be born into a new set of circumstances.

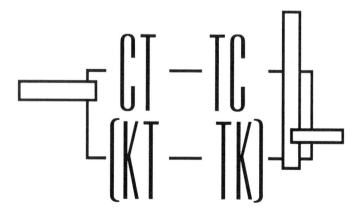

*Tick-tock** (TC-TK), the sound made by a clock, is a key work in this configuration. It is the rhythmic beat of time, which had its inception when

---

*Cf. *tachy* (TC as in *tachycardia*), beating fast, swift.

the immensity, identifying Itself with its own center (an inconceivable point of intensity), transformed Itself into something immeasurably small (K—the ultimate compression) and, crossing over into manifestation, burst into myriad aspects of Itself. Mythologically, these points of splendor were the germs in Pandora's box, which when opened spread dis-ease throughout the world. That is, they represent the instability of the manifested state, a state subject to the fluctuations of time. However, these points of splendor instinctively set into play the movement or heartbeat that seeks ever to return to the Source. It is the movement of Time, which orbits in a Universal Circle, beginning nowhere and ending nowhere.*

Once time is born, the years and the months and the days, the hours and the minutes and the seconds, are subdivided many times over, the subdivisions of time being like the sands of the sea. These subdivisions provide the framework of history. Time weaves its magic web, and losing sight of the whole, man becomes enmeshed in the parts.† He becomes time-bound, a victim of time or the whirling (cf. worlding) of the Absolute.

The Absolute, by casting itself into the mold of time, becomes sheathed or covered (cf. *theca*‡ as sheath). Several TC-CT words refer to shelter, container, cover: *tick* (cloth filled with cotton, etymologically related to theca), *thick* (related esoterically to theca as dense cover), *tectrix* (wing covert of a bird), *tuck* (as in tucking in a child), *tectum* (rooflike structure or covering), *tectonics*§ (the constructive arts–thus *technique, technology,*

---

*The Universe as we know it (existence as opposed to istence or the thing-in-itself) can be symbolized as a great clock, because anything that is manifested is subject to time. The word *clock* can be broken down into *c-lock,* or the locked up C. This can be interpreted to mean that the C, or third letter of the alphabet, is locked up or imprisoned in time. Another way to put it is that the third force potential—eternity—is concealed in time, hidden in the present moment, the elusive now. But a complementary meaning can be that the K force (the sound of C in *clock* is K) or the compressing power of life is wound up in a clock, which when released generates the pulse or the mark of time. That is, the locking up of the Absolute's potential in time (the ki or life energy is limited) makes life possible on earth and sets off the primal heartbeat.

†Part backwards reads t-r-a-p: to be identified with anything less than the whole is to fall into a trap!

‡*Theca* is basically TC. The affixing of an H emphasizes enclosure.

§The essence of tectonics is weaving, sheltering, covering.

*textile,) coat, cote, cottage, cuticle* (outer cover), *cot* (in one denotation, small shelter), *cotton* (out of which cloth is made).

Related to *cover* is the concept of descent, down, for what is on the bottom is grounded, covered by dense growth. (cf. hell—the descent of the spirit to Stygean darkness). This principle generates words such as *catacomb, catastrophe, cataclysm, catabolism, catachresis* (misuse of a word), *cation,* and *cataclastic* (broken down).

The word *cat* (*Felis catus*) is also related to the prefix *cata-,* for since ancient times the cat has symbolized either a god or a devil. It thus stands for that principle that can turn against itself and "descend" (cata) into the netherworlds or infernal regions where darkness reigns supreme. The cat sees in the dark, possesses nine lives (that is, renews itself like the gods), and is often the familiar of witches. It is also known for its aloofness, being in the world—the devil—but not of it—the god. It is also an expert mouse catcher, which is to say that the principle of light (the cat as god) in its capacity to penetrate the darkness (become a devil) is capable of overcoming man's instinctive timidity, his mouselike nature. *Cat* reversed reads *tac,* the root of *tacit* (silence). The cat is *"in touch with"* the Source of all life, that silence which surpasses understanding. (It is like the bee, which when in touch with the nectar stops buzzing!) Consider in this connection the word *tact,* in essence meaning "to be in touch with" the Source, thus the gracefulness and delicate manner.

In a paradoxical way, the prefix *cata-* (down) undergoes purification. It is raised up through the process of CT-KT (dying to oneself and scattering seed); thus the words *catharsis, Catherine, cathartic,* and *Cathar.*

Once man, as creature, has descended (cf. *cut,* CT, separated from or cut off from the Source), he awakens to find himself in a time-bound world. Having lost sight of the whole, he catches as catch can, holding on for dear life, forgetting that in essence he has nowhere to fall. This gives rise to the CT word *catch* and the TK word *take* (to seize, grasp, also to *kite* (KT), a greedy, grasping person. Something *tacky* (TC-TK) is sticky (holding on to), and a *tack* is used to affix. Indeed, the word *touch** is related, for to *catch* something or to *take* it is to be in *touch* with it. If there is no TK process

---

*Touch is basically TC, the H serving to soften the K sound. *Touch* is etymologically related to the Vulgar Latin *toccare,* which in all probability is derived from *tok,* a light blow (cf. *tocsin* with the clapper *touching* the bell).

(the pouring of the empty into a mold, K), nothing can be opposed to itself and therefore nothing can be in touch. Thus the word *kith* (KT, a friend or acquaintance), one who is close to you, or in touch. The word *tax* (tacks, TC-TK) is etymologically related to *touch*. (Cf. the expression, "How much did he touch you for?) Esoterically, it is the payment one makes to be in touch with this world. The word *tacit* is also related esoterically to *touch*, for if one is in touch with this source he is *tacit*.

Adam/Eve descended (TK) after eating of the Tree of Knowledge of Good and Evil. Thus TK is related to knowledge, or penetration into one's own profundity. This generates *acuteness* (CT-KT), or sharpness, and *couth* (CT), or refinement. It turns one into a *teacher* (TC-TK), one who can grasp (take hold of) the meaning, or catch on. The goal of this TC-TK process is the paradoxical renewal of the Absolute, which is elegantly illustrated by the following TK words: *tyke* (child, the renewed Spirit), *tocology* (obstetrics), and *Tiki* (the Polynesian primal man).

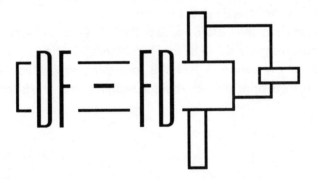

The key concept in this pairing is nourishment (FD, *food, feed, fed, fodder*). The inevitable opposite, DF (*duff*), generates decay. D is the door of manifestation through which life enters and death exits. The F serves as power source, energizing and joining with the D.

In *fides,* there is trust, faith, a building up or nourishing process (cf. *confide*). But then there is also *doff* (DF), to be thrust aside, and *deaf* (to be cut off), the prefix *dif* as in differ (away, apart) *fade* and the combining form *fid* (split or separated into, as in *palmatifid*), *daffy* (crazy, split apart, not connected), *fad* (a fashion that is soon cut off and fades).

The opposites merge in the word *feud* (FD), which means at once land (cf. *feudal*)—that which provides nourishment—but also *enmity* (to have a *feud*) which is related to destruction or casting out.

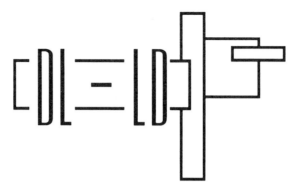

DL, poetically rendered, is the Lost Light or the Son of Man (L, the elevated one) buried in manifestation (D). Thus *dull* (not bright, earthy), *dual* (the division characterizing earthy man), *dole* (division or portion, as in *deal*—but also sorrow—the earthy condition or dark night of the soul), *doll* (in one of its older denotations meaning *dung*).* A *dolly* is a vehicle for the transportation of heavy objects (earthy, claylike, a *load*—LD). A *dell* or *dale* is a valley (hollowed out of the earth).

In *load, lead* (the metal), and *lade* the L, likely to be found in low places, is further weighted down by the D (existence). *Lad* in its original sense was a man of low station. A *lid* holds something down. *Lady* pertains to the female, earth principle—the burden bearer, or she who is *laden* with child.

---

*To connect *dung* with the playthings of little children may sound preposterous, but surely many of the dolls primitive children played with were made of clay, the *duff* or *dung* of the earth. Consider, in this frame of reference, the word *idol*. Etymologically, the word has nothing to do with *doll*, but esoterically it certainly does, for i-dol is the worship of the ego or I in the form of an icon or doll.

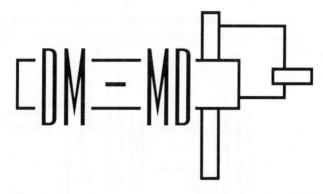

M and D together (in one sense, water, M, and earth, D) generate the word *mud,* which is a mixture of both. To be *mad* is to be earthbound, unduly influenced by the material condition. To be *made* is to undergo this process of formation (the mixture of earth and water: "Dust thou art and to dust returnest"). Even *maid,* as female, serves creation by giving birth to a child—that which is made. The conjunction MD establishes *mood* (cf. *mode*), or mental disposition—how we respond to our material condition or state of being. In *mid, mod, med (middle, mediate, meditate, moderate, mode)* we are at the center or halfway mark (cf. *demi,* DM). One side of the equation is matter and the other, spirit, and when the equation is solved their equivalency is revealed. The house of God (cf. *dome* and *domicile,* DM) is situated in the *midst* of all this mud. "The center is everywhere, the circumference nowhere."

*Dame* as female (cf. *maid*) is the mother, or earth principle. *Dim* and *dumb* illustrate the obfuscation brought about by this muddling or meddling (mixing). *Dome* (referring poetically to a stately structure or mansion) suggests the basic, underlying mudlike construction of primitive buildings. Mastery of this earthy element, *domination* of it (*dom,* master) is the task set for earthbound man. The peril, however, is to be stuck at the other end of the stick: to be struck *dumb*—overwhelmed by the clay instead of mastering it. To be identified with that half of life is to be *doomed\** (cf. *demon*).† Damn falls into the doom category, but paradoxically (as in *daemon*), to *dam up*

---

*\*Doom* is also destiny, that which is laid down or fated.
†*Demon* is also *daemon*—the creative genius

is also a way to create power and energy. With the proper alchemical attitude, the mud of manifestation can be transmuted to *mead,* for the potential (in MD) is there.

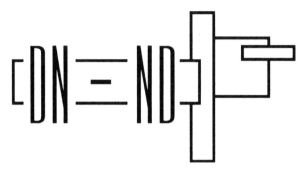

This combination refers to the death (D) or descent of the Spirit (N) into manifestation, that which is made, crystallized, or *done.* Consider also the following words: *down, node* (knotted, compressed), *nidify* (lay down a nest), *den, dun* (drab, gloomy), *dung, dunk, dingy, dank, deign* (descend), *dent, nadir, nod* (sleep), *need* (the "desert" of material life), *nude* (cf. need), *deny* (to do without).

But for all the storm and stress of that descent, the rewards are also great, for manifestation is how man develops his potential and concentrates his power. Consider, for example, the following power words: *dean* (originally chieftain of ten); *deni* (cf. *denary*), from the Latin meaning "ten," encompassing within its scope existence (1) and non-existence (0); *Don* (master); *dyne* (power); *node* (point of concentration); *deny* (a yogic device for concentrating power).

As with most other configurations down can also mean up! For example, the word *downs* means open, high, grassy land. To *dine* is to be nourished, raised up.

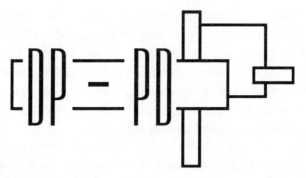

With D symbolizing the physical and P active penetration, the word *deep* picturesquely describes the thrust into manifestation, and *dip* and *dope* the resulting stupefaction. To *dupe* is to deceive, bring down (cf. *drop* and *droop,* where the R as will intensifies the sense of DP).

Depth of penetration (PD) also implies foundation, base, and support, as in the common use of the prefix *ped-* (foot, as in *pedestrian,* or child—the foundation of the man—as in *pediatrics. Pod* also refers to foot (*podiatry*) or seed vessel—the foundation or support of the seed. A *pad,* besides pertaining to the concept of foot (walking), also signifies cushion (support).

Before Adam and Eve were cast out of the Garden of Eden, there was no differentiation of color. But once man fell into duality he became *pied* (PD). Black and white both became evident and later exploded into Joseph's coat of many colors (Genesis 37:3).*

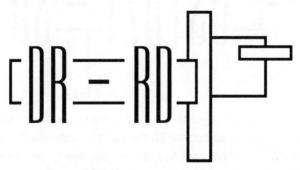

The configuration DR-RD (where D represents concrete force and the physical, and R will and strength) tends to generate words that emphasize

---

*Recall that Joseph descended into Egypt, the land of darkness.

these aspects: *durable* (cf. *endure*), *dour* (hard),* *dare* (brave opposition), *dear* (archaic for hard, severe; also, precious, derived from the concentration of life energy, as in a diamond). In *dire* (cf. *dread*), the negative, fearful aspect of the crystallized condition is stressed. *Dry* derives from an Indo-European root meaning firm or solid. Consider also *dray* (cart that carries a heavy load), *drive* (force to go, push forward), *door* (by means of its symbolic strength it bars and permits entry).

In the following words the force of will (R)—to move ahead—is stressed, while the D provides the ground for it. A *road* is a means of providing movement. A *rudder* controls the direction of movement. *Red* is a violent movement or agitation (cf. *ruddy, rude*). *Ready* implies preparation to move; to *ride* is to be moved in a vehicle; to be *rid* of something is to have it removed; to *raid* is to rush into with deliberation; to *read* [†] (in this connection) is to move along the lines of a written passage; a *rod* (in one of its denotations) is a measure of length; *reed* derives from an Indo-European base meaning to shake, tremble (probably from the movement of the reeds in the wind). A *rood* in one of its denotations is a measure of length; in another (as cross), it refers to the movement of the soul into a higher dimension (from the horizontal D to the vertical R.)

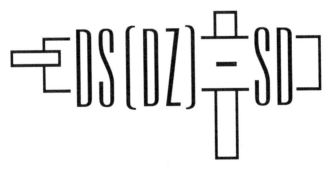

D represents our life on earth, and S the energy that transmutes it. Thus a *seed* is a concentrated code with the built-in potential for transmutation and development. This concentration of the life force can weigh a thing down, as in the following words: *sod, sodden, sad* (weighed down emotionally), *sediment, solder* (with a silent L, derived form a root meaning to

---

*Dour also means *gloomy* (cf. *dreary*), for imprisonment in matter is not only confining but depressing.

[†]*Rede* is advice: how to proceed and move along the pathway of life.

make solid), *sedentary, suds* (dregs, now obsolete), *sudra* (the lowest Hindu caste), *sudd* (obstructive masses of floating vegetable matter), *said* (already uttered, crystallized).

DS or DZ words tend to reflect the same heavy magnetic effect of the physical as SD words. For instance: *doss* (sleep), *dizzy, doze, daze.* Consider also the prefix *dis-* (to separate, as in *disjoin*), characteristic of the divided consciousness experienced on earth. (The SD word *side,* in one of its denotations, also refers to division.)

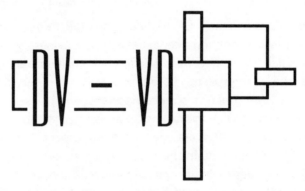

The words *dive* and *devil*\* illustrate the penetration of the V and the physical aspect of the D. For *dive* implies digging in, and the *devil,* often depicted with a goat-like V-shaped head for being identified with the sensual, likes to dig in. Yet there is the Hindu word *deva* (god) with the same DV root (cf. the Latin *diva* and the English *divine*), for it symbolically represents that aspect of the deity who steals the sacred fire and descends to earth. (Note the word *div-ide*: the fragmentation or death of the gods.)

In *video* (from the Latin *videre,* to see) one sees or penetrates (cf. *invade*). The word *void,* in this connection, suggests the utmost penetration to that which is empty or does not yet exist.

---

\*Note the relationship between *devil* and *develop* (devil-op). There would be no development for man except for his involvement with the devil. Thus his fall (cf. *diabolus,* thrown across). Strange that the bird of peace, the *dove,* suggests this involvement or penetration, for that, paradoxically, is where peace is to be found—in the *div-ided* (cf. piece, fragment) fragmented state. This is not to imply that peace is to be found in fragments, but through the fragmentation process (the breaking up of the whole into pieces) man reintegrates (re-members) himself, transmuting the fragment (piece) into the whole (peace).

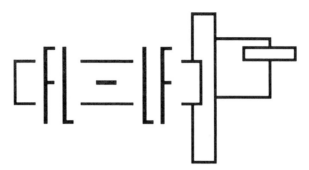

Such words as *fell*,* *fall*, *full*, *fill*,† *flop*, *foul*, *foil*, *flump*, *flunk*, and *flag* (as verb) all have in common a certain gravity, a heaviness, whereas the words *flew*, *fly*, *flee*, *flame*, *flue*, *flair*, *flip*, *flick*, *lift*, *luff* (wind) are lighter and tend to rise. The L expresses this up-down polarity, the F serving as intensifier.

The word *life* contains both components within itself. Superficially it appears to emphasize the raising up aspect (*lofty*). However, when read backwards (*efil*, *evil*), it assumes a different aspect. From the qabbalistic point of view, life contains hidden within it an evil or devil—that which compels us to desire. In life one has to wrestle continually with this devil/angel, and depending on the circumstances we are sometimes on top and sometimes on the bottom. Therefore, it is incumbent upon us to become aware of a third force that transcends both good and evil, for neither angel nor devil will release us from the servitude of a split consciousness.

To understand *life*, then it is first necessary to realize that you are both the highest and the lowest. If this equation can be balanced within us, then our greater light (E, the Light of God) will be joined (F) to his lesser light (I, or individualized light, commonly known as the ego). No attribute of life, then, whether it be good, evil, or any of the other countless polarities, can be identified with or fixated upon, for in that attempt the quality of life becomes impoverished.

---

*Note the similarity in sound between *phallus* (fallus) and *fall*, suggesting a relationship between the fall of man and desires (phallus).
†Cf. *fill* to *philo* (as in *philosophy*, from the Greek *philos*, loving). To be filled with the Spirit is to love.

Therefore, the word *life* can be rendered thus:

L, that which rises and falls (the Tree of Knowledge of Good and Evil).

I, by itself the ego or the individualized I, identified with one thing or another.

F, however, there is within us all a unifying power.

E, that can join us to the greater light, which is the power to see the Tree of Knowledge of Good and Evil as it really should be seen—as the Tree of Life.*

Therefore, life is the pulsation (L, the breathing in and the breathing out, the rise and the fall, the creation and the destruction) of that grand organism that is the all and everything. The greater light (E) emerging from the center becomes the lesser light (I) as it moves towards the circumference. But the power of unity (F) joins these two lights (Good and Evil, or the redemption of Adam) to create a circulation that can be likened to the movement of blood in the grand organism, its involutionary and evolutionary thrust.

To *feel* is to make contact (cf. the action of a *file*) or to move toward. Here the L puts us in touch with the basest as well as the most lofty parts of ourselves (the higher E-motions, or that light, E, which moves us, or toward which we move).

A divine Fool is filled with the Spirit, for he is in touch with the highest (L) and the lowest (also L). A lowercase fool is filled only with hot air.

The Fool of the Tarot is the divine Fool whose number is Zero. Like the Joker he can become any card, for he is the highest and the lowest and everything in between for the sole reason that he is identified with Nothing (0).

---

*The E is the silent activator, lighting up the I (cf. bit to bite, sit to site, kit to kite). The addition of the greater light, E, activates the lesser light, I. Its presence rekindles or wakes up the sleeper, and their equivalency is acknowledged.

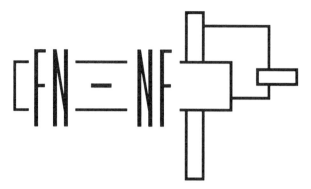

The key word in this configuration is the Hebrew word *Nefesh* (soul), where N stands for the Spirit and F for all that is joined to it. (FN-NF can also be understood to convey esoterically the force, F, or impact of Spirit, N) The English cognates are many: *fana* (annihilation: the Spirit as nothing, cf. *Nirvana*\*), *fan* (related to wind, Spirit), *fun* (qabbalistically, an abbreviated form of *fundamental;* real fun is the enjoyment of basic spiritual values, a dipping into the *fund* of human experience). Stemming from the idea of basic or ground (*fundamental, font*) is the word *fen,* lowland. *Fine* means *finished* (FN) or brought to perfection, which brings out the essential qualities of a thing. *Fin* is a balance mechanism (that which centers, the source of our strength). Surely our Spirit is just that. A *knife* (NF) is a cutting edge (cf. *fang,* FN). *Enough* (*i-nuf*) is derived from an Indo-European base meaning to attain or achieve. (Cf. *final, found,* FN.) A *fane* is a temple, the material vehicle of the Spirit (*Nef,* cf. *nave*). *Faint* is esoterically related to *fana* (annihilation), and *fain,* strangely enough, means *eager* or *glad;* that is, a perfected soul is eager to move toward the annihilation of self. *Nifty* (NF) probably derives from mag-*nif*-icent, meaning great or enjoyable, as related to the Spirit.

---

\*Nirvana means *to blow out,* which is to extinguish, annihilate, be as nothing. It also means to exhale, to let go and therefore be released. It can also be interpreted to mean "to project"—the realization that this entire creation was "blown out" of *you,* that *you* are the Creator!

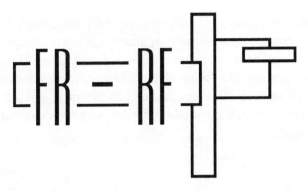

*Free* is a key word in this configuration, which essentially expresses the force (F) of the will (R). To be free is to move like the spider without becoming identified with (stuck on) any one part of the web (part reversed spells trap). The free soul is at home at the center and the circumference, coming and going in peace.

FR words, because of this movement of the R to and from the center, tend to be intense: *fire, fierce, fury, fry, fervor, foray, force, pharaoh* (he who moves toward the center). But the R also moves away from the center and distances itself from it, as in the following FR words: *far, further, freeze, fur* (extending out from the surface), *roof* (outer covering of a house—cf. *rafter*), *reef* (thrust out from the water), *rough* (*ruff*)—the outermost cover tends to be unrefined, tough, as it is the furthest removed from the influence of the center (cf. *ruffle, raffish, riffraff*). A *raft* (RF) floats on the surface but also *ferries* (FR) passengers to and from the center. *Rift* is a separation from unity. The word *rife* indicates what is current (central), thrust before you, evident, or not hidden. A *frame* is an outermost covering. *From* often means point of origin, as opposed to end point. Here, as in other RF-FR words, the concepts of near and far coincide in the same configuration. As has been said, the word *free* is an excellent example of this coincidence of opposites.*

---

*In the word before the sense of near and far also coincide. *Before* can denote the *past* (before I was born), the present (*before* me stands...) and future (the life of a child lies *before* him). Consider also the word *for:* as prefix it means (1) away, apart, off (as in *forbid, forget, forgo*), or (2) very much, intensely (*forlorn, forworn*). Thus it is illustrative of both the sense of distance (*far*) and nearness (intensity),

*Feral* means untamed, wild, removed from the center. *Fer,* as suffix (cf. *Lucifer, conifer,* means bearer, producer. Lucifer is the light-*bearer,* carrying with him the consciousness of the will that hurled him (cf. diaballein, to throw across) into the confines of this world. (Cf. *ferry* and *fare*— the price of transition.) The process of FR-RF is *feracious* (fruitful)* and *fertile* because it conceals the subtle design of our existence: that which moves out of itself.

---

characteristic of FR-RF. *For* as preposition is used in many different ways, but its sense of purpose and design is of special interest, as in "What is life *for?"* It's as if we ask, "What is this will to be? How is this desire for existence, for movement of the soul, to be channeled, directed?" Eternity *is;* time *moves.* The word *for* straddles both time and eternity, for at its center it is motionless but at the periphery it whirls like a cosmic clock. In this connection, consider the word *fear* (FR). One who is truly afraid instinctively freezes and becomes paralyzed. He cannot move at all. (Cf. the ostrich burying its head, the opossum playing dead, the schizophrenic's catatonia.) Once the soul (in evolution) moves away from the center, it may sense this dread of alienation instinctively (cf. *fear* and *far*). Movement involves change, but change can be traumatic as well as challenging, hence conflict. (Cf. the story of the prodigal son.) Movement away from the center (toward individuation) creates *friction.*

(FR, cf. *frayed* and *fret:* rubbed off), which by its own nature creates heat and fire, reducing the "runaway" to ashes or essence again. Thus, to be truly an adept of the FR-RF process, to be truly *free,* one must move out from the center—yes—but on moving out must realize that the friction (opposition, duality of the divided state, center vs. circumference, deity vs. devil) has a built-in safety mechanism and that all the dross created by the expulsion from the Garden(cf. the FR word *fart,* to blow out wind) will be consumed by that very process—the will of man— that enticed it to leave in the first place. When all this is taken into consideration, the word *fortune* (for-tune) can be understood to mean to be in tune with these forces that move one's life, or simply to be in tune with *for.*

*How close to *ferocious!* Once more the coincidence of opposites, the fruit of man being made in the midst of fire.

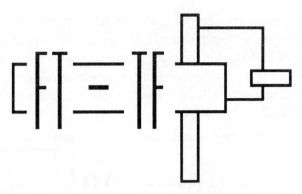

FT-TF refers to a concentration (F) of life at the growing point (T). Thus the words *fat* (weighty), *fate* (the weight of destiny, cf. *future*), *foot* (weight-bearer), and *fetter* (weigh down). A *fete* is a gathering together, a joyous concentration to celebrate life. A *flight* (FT) is a concentration of force (cf. *feat, tiff, tough, toffy, tufa, tuft*). To feel *fit* is to enjoy the concentration of life in you, but to be subject to *fits* is to upset the delicate balance.

This concentration of life at a point (FT) is admirably illustrated in the words *fetus* and *photo* (from *foto,* light). Consider also *phyto,* that which emerges from the concentrated essence of the seed substance. *Father* is the concentration of seed power. *Faith* is confidence in that power that emerges from istence to existence through the growing point.

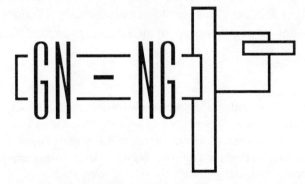

The N (spirit—nothing, never, cessation of activity, darkness) coupled with the G (interior movement, organic transformation) generates such words as *Negro, negate, neglect* (nothing done), *nag* (a nagging thought *gnaws* at you, usually from an obscure corner of the mind, demanding attention because it has been *neglected*), *nog* (a strong ale that "eclipses" the self (cf. *gin*—GN). In GN the spirit or seed-substance (N), which contains the germ, undergoes organic transformation (G) and as such can be eclipsed, as in *goon* and *gone** (the burial of the seed, its disappearance; cf. *negate,* NG), or activated, as in *generate, gonad* (and other *gono-* words), *genius, gene, gun* (the explosive quality of the buried seed), *Agni* (the god of fire— the living "germ," the flame of life; cf. *igneous*), *gain, gyn* (woman as generator), *begin* (to "generate").

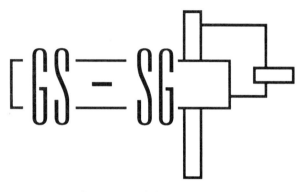

With the G as organic transformer, and the S as burning, or transmuting, there is a general reinforcement in this pairing, which generates such words as *gas†* and *gust*. This baring of essence by the transformation process generates words like *gist* (bearing on the main point) and *gestation* (relating to growth). In *gustatory,* taste is developed and food is rolled on the tongue, the instinct being to contemplate its transformation. There is an implicit sense of delight in this process of intake and absorption. To *guess* (GS) is

---

*Cf. *gonio* (angle) and *gon* (as in polygon—many angles). An *angle* is the shape made by two straight lines meeting in a point. (Thus the narrowing as the lines converge; the two lose their identity at the point. It is "gone"—*gon*.) This narrowing down (coming together) is a function of NG. Thus *gen*—to come together, as in *gens* (clan), *genus,* and *gentle* (cf. the related word *join*).

†The word *gas* was invented by Van Helmont but nevertheless conforms to the patterning. Actually, every word we use was invented. And when we think agout it even man was invented. (God, too, someone will say!) The Ungrund expresses itself as a God, devil, or alphabetic sound—actually anything it wants to be. God doesn't so much invent or create the world but *acts* it (as the Hindus are fond of saying). So Van Helmont "acted" gas just as Kasner's son "acted" googol!

to catch something on the wind (or spirit, cf. *ghost, gas*), and then to mull it over. A *guest* is someone appearing at the door with the wind. *Goose* as simpleton (a silly goose) is probably a degeneration of the sacred status held by the goose in antiquity as a sun bird venerated for its fertility. As such, more than just an ordinary simpleton or silly person, it symbolizes the Divine Fool, always *gasing* (transforming, making life fertile). To "goose" someone (a playful rear-end prod) may well be reminiscent of these ancient fertility festivals.

These GS-SG words reflect aspects of digestion either literally or figuratively. Their key consonants (the S as *Shin*—tooth—and the G as gut or conveyor), indicate transformation. Thus a *sage* is one who can undergo this transformation. A *siege* is a cutting off and surrounding, so that instead of food, now the enemy (also, like a food, a foreign body) can be assimilated. Likewise, a *segment* is a piece cut off—the part to be digested. *Sag* and *sog* suggest a general heaviness, for the matter to be transformed suffers from the drag (cf. *dregs*) or weightiness of manifestation. *Sig* (urine) is one of the end products of this transformation, and *sigmoid* (S-shaped) twists gutlike in its function of transformation. The word *geist* (as in *zeitgeist*), meaning spirit, is the beginning and end of that transformation. *Guise* (GS), as manner of dress, appearance (and so deceiving) is the mistlike "mayavic" form the spirit assumes.

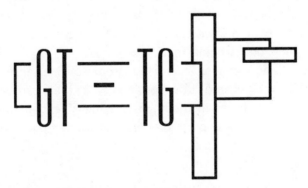

The G, moving toward and enfolding itself, when conjoined to the T, provides a channel through which life enters and emerges. Food moves through the *gut;* one enters or leaves through a *gate*. In *getting* (GT), one brings in something material or immaterial for which an exchange is made in kind. In *begetting,* a child is born of the process (G is the enveloping womb and T the emerging child).* A *goat* can be characterized as a personified gut, as it is capable of digesting coarse food. As scapegoat it receives our coarseness.) *Gita* means *song*† (as in the *Bhagavad-Gita,* the Song of the Blessed One), which when inspired originates on a gut level (G) emerging (T) through the instrumentality of sound. *Gait* originally referred to a path between two hedges (cf. *gut*). *Tog, toga, tegmen, integument* all relate to cover, that which enfolds. Likewise, *tag,* originally a hanging end of a garment.) *Gut* backwards is *tug*—to pull, drag—which suggests the food being conveyed through a peristaltic gut.

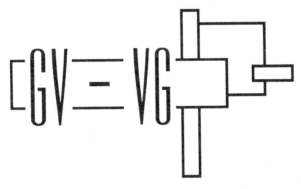

The key word in this configuration is *give*. The secret of giving is to give *all,*‡ which is the secret of life itself, for that which bestows the gift of life can do so only by sacrificing self—by emptying itself conpletely into its creation. Only in this way does the Creator become the created: not by holding back, but by being That.

V is penetration, digging in, and the essence of G is transformation. The life spirit, by moving into its own profundity (for there can be nothing outside of it), by exploring the depth of its being (V) experiences a transformation (G) that can be expressed as its gift to life, or—put more philosophically—its gift to itself.

---

*Gyte* is an obsolete word for child.

†*Song* or *Son* (sound) of G or sound of the gut transmuted through art.

‡In tithing, one-tenth is all that is required. The word tithe derives from *ten,* which is the number of completion that contains all. It is only an illusion, but a powerful one, that one can give partially. It is either all or nothing.

Thus the words *vigor* (VG)—that which enlivens (cf. *vigil*) and *vegeta-tive*—alive, growing, plantlike.

In *vago* (nerve), as in *vagus*, the spirit wanders (cf. *vagabond, vagary, vague*), branches out nervelike in all directions, in order to sensitize and innervate the furthest reaches of manifestation.

It is interesting to note that *gyve* (GV) means shackle or fetter. The *gyv-ing* or *giving* of one's life also binds it,* for as with Christ, the giving of one's life as a gift to mankind involves one in the mystery of binding (crucifix-ion). It is a mystery of such scope that once it is revealed (opened) it is immediately reveiled (closed).

The word *vogue* means in fashion, or that which emerges transformed form the depth or the Source of all life.

---

*To *bind* is to hold tight or grasp. The verb to give is probably derived from the Indo-European base *ghabh*, to grasp, take (related to the Latin *habere*—to have). Thus, to give all expresses an impossible paradox, the giving up of one's freedom too, and this *binds* the Spirit, Prometheus-like, to the world of matter or to the world of its projected Self.

The Indian *bindu* is the dark "drop" of light, the Absolute reduced to a point of intensity (cf. Tsimtsum). It is the Seed of potential freedom, the locked-up essence of life.

Etymologically, the English word *gift* can be traced back to the Germanic *gift*, meaning *poison*! Thus the *gift* of life one receives can be viewed esoterically as a poison (cf. the ancient oxygen in the atmosphere—the gift of life—as a poison), which binds Prometheus to the Rock of Ages. In the act of losing his life (being poisoned, or being "de-livered" by Simurgh) he finds it again (is "delivered")! Thus, this bondage (giving as grasping) is the other face of one's freedom.

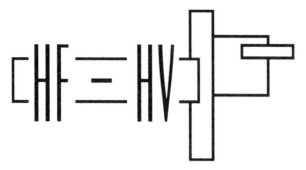

H encloses or possesses, and V digs in. To *have** implies just this. A *heavy* object, bound by its own weight, impresses itself on substance. (The self—H—drags us down.) A *haven* is a sheltered, enclosed place (cf. *hive* and *hovel*). A *haft* is a handle, which one can cling to grasp, possess. A *hoof* is a foot or claw that digs in. (The devil's cleft hoof symbolizes a split understanding that clings to possessions.) *Heaven* (related esoterically to *heavy*) has been raised—*heaved*—up and rendered light by the alchemist's art (cf. *hover*). *Havoc* signifies that which is possessed and dug in beyond redemption (destroyed by its own weight). *Half*† is generated by the concept of cutting (splitting, digging in). To *huff* is to blow or swell‡ with pride (which can be likened to *heave* and *hover*). *Hafiz* is an honorary title given to someone who has memorized the entire Koran; in other words, he has dug in (V) and possessed it (H).

---

*Eve*, the mother of all the living, elementary existence, life itself, is related (esoterically to *have* (*Eve*=*Havah* in Hebrew). An intuitive leap reveals that a man can possess (have, own) only his own life (*Eve, Havah*). But instead of a man possessing his life (*having* it) in the positive sense (he is one with it because he can have only what he is), he becomes possessed by it. (Note also the primitive concept of woman (*Eve, Havah*) as possession—that which is owned or *had, Havah*.

†Note the silent L in *half*: the Spirit (L), or whole, is concealed within the part, or half (HF). The *hal* of hal-f approximates the sound of *whole* and is related to it etymologically.

‡Cf. the swelled-up, raised surface of a *hive*.

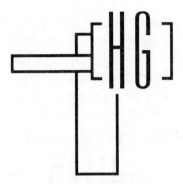

The H encloses, and the G, reinforcing this movement by its interior, gut-like activity, generates *hug,* an instinctive wraparound, as if preparing to ingest. A *hog* is a gluttonous, self-indulgent person, identified with his gut, while *huge* suggests the bulge of this primitive, instinctive force. A *hag* is a witch often characterized by her cannibalistic desires (cf. the witch in "Hansel and Gretel"). *Hag,* as verb, derives from a root meaning to cut, *hack* (pertaining to wood). (To *haggle* is to try to cut the price.) This is merely another aspect of the *hag* (as witch, harpy, demon) who cuts, hacks, fragments, dismembers for the sake of incorporation and self-enhancement. *Hegemony* is domination of one state over another (cf. the concept of incorporation—one state consuming another). *Hagio-* (holy) is incorporation in the highest sense, the re-membering of man, the realization of his Unity. This is the *hug* (HG) of the Almighty.

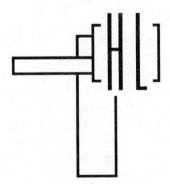

The H as fence, boundary, field of work, and the L as the life enclosed within it, together generate the word *Hell*—the binding (H) of the Lord (EL).* Like-

---

*Cf. *shell,* which is a cognate of *Sheol*—where the shells live.

wise, the word *hull* (outer cover) within which dwells the soul (L).

The restriction of the Absolute is a recurrent theme in all religious literature, and HL is a perfect vehicle for this expression. This conjoining, which
provides a home (H) for the spirit (L) can be likened to *holy**\* wedlock. It is
the essence of all *healing* (HL), for it integrates man, putting him in touch
with his lowest element (cf. *heel, hole,* and *hylo*—wood, matter) as well
as his highest (cf. *heal* and *helio*—sun, also *hill* and *whole*).

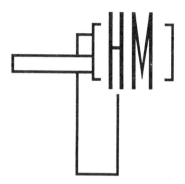

HM symnbolizes material (M) possession (H), that which is roped off or
enclosed for an indwelling spirit. Thus HM generates *home* and also *homo*†

---

\**Holy:* from *hole,* a hollowed-out place, an opening. It brings into play the mystery
of emptiness; yet, strangely, it is bound by the H. It is like a cup (cf. the Holy Grail),
the shape of which materializes the emptiness, draws it out. This is the hollow
(womb) in which man is conceived. Emptiness *per se* (the Void) is inconceivable.
To be seen—comprehended—it must be enclosed, thus holy. With the prefix W
it becomes *whole* (unified, integrated), for the W (which see) is a reciprocal
function, always referring the you (world) back to itself, bringing it together,
making it whole. The piercing of Christ, his being wounded—his vulnerability—
also sanctified him, made him holy. It was this sacrifice, paradoxically, that made
him whole. He was able to receive the slings and arrows of existence (cf. Mara's
onslaught of Buddha), the slaying in the world, which released his Spirit (the
uncorking of the bottle) and make him whole again. (Cf. the puncturing of the
earth—Christ's body—for the purpose of planting seeds. Out of that hollow, new
life arises: life which provides nourishment for all. Out of Christ's wound poured
the blood that fills the Grail, which provides spiritual nourishment for all. To use
but a slightly different analogy, as the cracked nut reveals the kernel, so the dying
self reveals the God, and man is raised up.)
†Cf. *him* (he who has received the Spirit).

(the vehicle or *home* for the soul). To *hem* means to enclose, to double back and confine; to *hum*\* is to sing with closed (enclosing) lips. The sound thereby produced is the sound of OM: the drone of material, locked-in existence, the sound inside a hive. The *ham* is the back or dark side, which is "hidden" or enclosed. Since blood is the life, *hemo* (cf. *hemoglobin*) is its vehicle in man.

P is to extend oneself, to push, to penetrate, to be active, while the H sets limits to the thrust of P, containing and directing it. (It is the resistance required for anything to take off!) Thus *hip* and *hop* (as related to leap—cf. *heap*), *hep* (incite to greater activity); *hup* (urge on a horse), and *hope* (a leap into the future, expectation). To *hype* is to stimulate, excite; likewise *hypo*[†] (from hypodermic). *Hyper* is above, over, more than the normal. In *hap*[‡] and *happen* there is the sense of bubbling up, activity, a leaping into being as if anything can *happen*. (Compare the closely related word *happy*, in its purest sense meaning being with it—whatever *happens*. *Hepato-* is a combining form meaning liver, the seat of life and activity (HP). In *hippo* the intense activity is centered in a horse, which often symbolizes the *emotions* (or the light—E—which drives us and makes us move. *Hoopla* is great excitement.

---

\*Cf. *hymn.*

†*Hypo* also means under, beneath, below, as opposed to *hyper*. (The thrust of P moves up and down.) In *hypno,* sleep, the N negates the activity.

‡*Hap* also means to cover; a *huppa* is a wedding canopy, and a *hoop* being bent back on itself forms an enclosure. In these three instances the H is stressed over the P. The activity is sheltered.

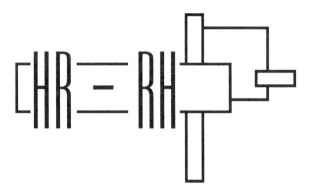

*Here* (HR) indicates either a pinpoint (to be *here*) or the universe itself (the *Here* for God).\* The H is an enclosure or circle, and the R is the radiating will to be. The soul, depending on its age, identifies with with either the part or the whole. To realize that the center† is everywhere and that the circumference is nowhere is to be *here now,* in the consciousness of the Absolute. To the grand man the little *here* of the toe and the little *here* of the heart are connected to the big *here* of his overall Being, albeit on the surface they may appear to be galaxies apart.

The *here,* then, is not only a point or center but can swell to the size of the entire universe. This is the consciousness of the *hero,* (HR), a being who realizes his relationship to the center as well as to the circumference, for he can *hear* the resonance of the One Sound (Logos) spoken by God, So to *hear* with absolute clarity (to have perfect pitch) is to know where one stands in relationship to the world—that *Thou Art That.* For to realize that you are *there* too is the precondition for realizing that you are also *here.*

*Hair* (HR) radiates from the center to the periphery like the rays of the sun. (Samson's *hair* was the sun's radiations.)

*Hour* (HR), *horal, horae, horology, horary, horoscope* all relate to time but also have an inner connection to *here*—that whatever the hour, now\*

---

\*Consider the word *there* (pointing away—what is *here* is not *there*). But concealed within t-here is here. In other words, through the magic of T—crossing over from one state of being to another—one realizes that here is there and there is here.

†Interestingly, a Japanese word for center is *hara* (HR).

‡*Now* is an interesting construction. The N, as spirit, dominates, while the 0 (Nothing) reinforces it. The W takes on its ancient meaning of *Waw,* to be joined

is the time. The *hour* is here. As an individual you fall under a particular influence, but to realize that you are also the All that projected the man is to fall under still another influence. The hour of your birth on whatever day of the year is equal to the breadth of your conception, for the will to be an individual is merely a subset of the will of the Absolute.

A root of the word *horizon* (HR) is *horos*—bounding circle, the field of work encompassing the here and now. (Cf. *hora*—dancing in a circle—like the *hours*.) *Horus* is the Egyptian sun god, the center of the circle, but also the extent (R) of his influence. Similarly, the *heart* * is the center of a person, a radiating sun (cf. all the branching blood vessels), and the *hearth* (HR) is the center of the home, radiating its warmth.

The use of the title *Herr* to denote gentleman (venerable, noble) smacks of the same primordial sense of being *here* now, of being a *hero*. It's like affixing a radiant sun to one's name.

A *whore* (HR—cf. *harlot*) is a personification of desire, and as such harks back to the original sin, whereby man desired "to taste of time"† and so *hurled* (HR) himself into the orbit of worlds (the Wheel of Fortune), where he became identified with his desires and lost sight of his true love, that which is here and now: time/eternity.

To the extent that we identify with time and *hours* instead of now, we experience the terror or *horror* (HR) of our situation, how *harmful* (HR) it is to us, and how we lose sight completely of our ancient potential for *harmony*.‡ If one understands the key to this configuration, the pattern of many of the other HR-RH words emerges. Thus, to *hurry* is to rush out (leave the center—cf. *hurl*). *Hoary* is very old, extended (R). A *horn* radiates out (like hair) from the head. *Harsh, harass,* and *harpy* (snatcher) relate in various shades

---

to, which in this particular instance is to be joined to NO-W or No Thing. So *Now* is *nowhere!* (the closest we come in our everyday lives to a timeless state)! Backwards it becomes *won*. The conjunction of time and eternity in *NOW* is at once a mark of victory—won—and unity—one. And anagrammatically *own* is generated. That is to say, to be in *Now* is to come into one's own!

*The *heart* is also a drum that sounds out (cf. *heard*) man's *hours* in this world.
†To taste of time or taste of the "hours"—cf. *houri*—a seductively beautiful woman—which suggests that man is seduced by "time." Also, compare *hour* to *whore,* and incidentally, *while* (referring to time) to *wile* (deceit).
‡Harm and harm-ony. Simply affix the N (Spirit) and balance is restored.

of meaning to *harm*—out on a limb, removed from the center, not being *here*. The HR-related army words, *harness* (originally referring to armor), *Harold* (leader of the army), *harbinger* (originally, a shelter for soldiers), *harbor* (army shelter), *herald* (army chief), *Hera* (Protectress), *Herbert* (bright army), simply reflect our source of strength—the will (R) to move out from the center to the circumference, or the limits or our world (H), and do battle. Another way of seeing it is that our source of strength is the *her\**—the *here* and *now*. In recognition of this, man shouts *hurray* and *hurrah*, expressions of wonder that he can move into his world and conquer. He can be compared to a diver sent after a precious pearl. To forget, even for a moment, that he is connected to his source by a lifeline is to experience *horror*.

To *hire* someone is to exchange salary for service. Ideally, the equation is balanced, and the flow out (wages) is equal to the flow in (work). HR is a record of movement out and movement back.

The other side of HR is RH, the root of *rheo-* (to flow, as in *rheostat, rheology,* and *rheophile*—living in flowing waters). *Rhea* is the mother of Zeus and the wife of Cronus (time). She is that which is emitted, flowing from the center of the wheel to the circumference. RH is that will to be, in time (cf. hour—Hr). *Rhetoric* is the flow of words; *rheum,* flowing discharge; *rhino,* nose flow (!); *rhizome,* creeping, flowing stem; *rhyme,* harmonious flowing—cf. *rhythm; rhodo-,* as rose, is that which rises up, flows out.

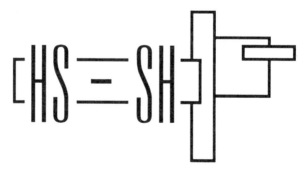

This combination, with the H as possessor (relating to self), and the S, also involved in possession—to transmute or to make one's own (recall the four

---

*\*Her,* referring to the feminine, is the ground (the place—H) of our being, the concentrated essence of the volitive faculty, where we willed to be (R) and where we are now (her-e). In other words, that's where the *here* is, hidden in the *her,* or the womb of the earth.

S's in *possess*), is ideal for generating such words as *his, has, house* (the sacred enclosure as possession—cf. *hospice, hostel, host. Hiss* is a warning to stay outside the sacred enclosure. (Cf. *hush*—to be quiet—to make oneself calm within that sacred space.) A *husk*, like a house, is a sheathing (cf. *hose*). In Yiddish, a *hozzer* is a pig—possessive (to eat like a hozzer). *Hostile* has the same sense of *hiss, hush* (cf. sh!)—that is, the enemy (the hostile one) is excluded from the sacred enclosure (HS).

Many *SH* words reinforce the conception of S as transmuting force and H as the magic circle or the territory of each individual ego. One might say for the sake of illustration that the SH represents the serpent caged, forced to live under confined and often severe conditions. Consider the following SH-dominant constructions implying a shutting off, a bounding, and therefore an excluding or casting out: *shit,*\* *shut, shackle, shave, shove* (to push out of one's territory), *shed* (as verb—to *shed* one's self), *shell, shuck, ship* (hollowed-out tree, enclosure), *shade* (excluding the sun, or as a ghost, having shed the mortal coil), *shore* (enclosing the sea), *Shiva* (the God of destruction, casting out), *Sheol* (the land of shades), *shy* (withdrawn into one's own circle of self—cf. *shun, shrink*), *shoo!* (similar to sh! and comparable to *hiss*, which is to invoke the sacredness of the magic circle), *shoot* (in one denotation to send forth). The words *shudder, shake, shimmy, shatter*, and *shriek* echo the fear of the *shearing* or cutting off process whereby one is left as an isolated ego defending his own circle, hole in the ground, or turf. This is the primal *shock*.

*She* symbolizes the feminine, the enclosing womb from which man is cast out (sh—a cutting off, *shearing*). In *shame*† one is uncovered, exposed, dragged out from under the protective enclosure of self. But just as friction generates, this focusing of the Absolute fire generates *shine, Shekinah* (the covered presence of God), *shah*, and *sheik* (rulers).

---

\*Cf. *ash* (SH)—that which is cast out after burning (also, *trash*). A strange Hebraic cognate, *aish* (aleph, yod, shin) means "intellectual man," that is the cast-out light!
†Cf. *shem*, which in Hebrew means *name*. That is the name is a cover, the clothes (cf. *close*) that label a man.

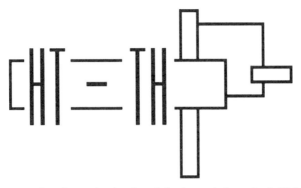

The two consonants that form the body of *the* have left an indelible mark on Western history. The T is the Tau or cross, while the H is the self that is affixed to it. *The,* as definite article (like the A as indefinite), lends the grandeur of God (*The-o*) to every object. To say *the boy* is to endow him with divinity. We all sense that holiness pervades everything, and language confirms this with the common usage of *A* and *The*.

The affixing of the self to the cross (crucifixion) symbolizes an individuating process where consciousness is brought to a point of concentration, with the meeting of the vertical (eternity) and horizontal (time) lines. The soul emerges as an individual, yet an individual who realizes that he/she is undivided (cf. in-dividual or "not divisible").

Thus the words *the, this, that, thee, thy, those, them, thou, they,* and *their* move toward specificity.* A *thing* is specific, and to *think* involves analysis, a breaking down into components (thing-ing). *Thank* can be seen esoterically as TH-ank (H). The ankh ( ☥ ) (crux ansata) is a symbol of eternity (the loop) affixed to time (the cross), which is another form of TH. Thus, to give thanks is to acknowledge the process that transmutes the Universal Spirit into a *thinking* being. (Cf. *Thoth,* the Egyptian god of learning and wisdom: a pure distillation of TH! TH is the penetration of life into every obscure corner of the Universe to make it intelligent. For that we give

---

*The* is a direct article, while A is indirect. Therefore, TH is individualized, specific, whereas A is universal. *The* book is designated as such, while *a* book can be any book. The cardinal number *four* is changed to the ordinal fourth by the addition of TH. That is to say, the four (a generalized concept) is individualized into a specific number, the fourth.

*thanks,* and to identify God (*The-o*) with this process is to acknowledge the process of individuation.

The other side of TH (HT) illustrates the same principle but in a different way. Here, a life force or heat is generated when the soul (cf. sole—single, only) undergoes the timing (taming) process. Thus we have the words *heat, hot, hit* (impact generating heat), *hate* (rage—full of heat), *hat* (a cover to conserve the heat), *hut* (likewise to conserve the heat), and *hoot* (to cry out in irritation). Mythologically, HT can be seen as Prometheus (T) bound (H), the life force under bondage bursting into flame.

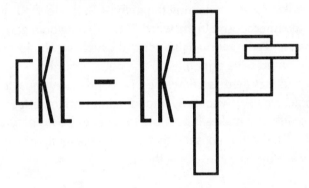

The compressing (K) of the light (L) to the point of snuffing it out generates the word *kill.* (Cf. *Kali*—black—the Hindu goddess who both creates* and destroys life.) *Coal* (KL) is compressed (K) plant matter containing within itself the light (L) of prehistoric lives. *Kohl*† is crushed (K) or powdered antimony. To *cull* is to gather together (K). The *keel* is the pressure bearer.

This snuffing out, locking up, shutting off, winding down, or pressing

---

*Another example of the linguistic phenomenon known as the identity of opposites. KL also creates, for the K as mold is womb to the fecundating light of L. *Kallos* (Greek for beauty, as in *kaleidoscope* and *calisthenics*) is related esoterically to *kill,* for to slay the self is to release the soul of beauty. And so *caliph,* from *Khalafa*—to succeed.

†Etymologically, the work *alcohol* derives from *al-kohl,* or "dark blue" (from the color of kohl). Esoterically, add god (AL), and we have alcohol as the dark blue god (or more poetically, the black god). As alcohol is the product of fermentation, so is the god, fermented of rotting selves. He/she has transmuted all the dark substances into blue light.

together is evident in many KL-LK words: *lock, coil, collar, collide, color* (from "to conceal"), *close, clamp, clutch, clap, cling, clay, clod* (cf. klutz), *climb* (from "to cling"), *clump, clew, clique, click, clot, claim, cloth, clam, clan, clasp, class, clench, claw, clip, clogged, cluster, calculus* (stone), *caul* (cover), *caulk, callus, kilo* (one thousand, thus, heavy, pressed together).

In *loka* (world, universe) and *locus* (place), the molding power of K on the most high (L) is nicely exemplified. In *luck,* one's fortune (light—*luc*— *luck*) is molded and bent into shape by the KL process. *Loki,* the god of mischief and discord, reflects this play of K and L.* A *lake* is nature's mirror (cf. *looking* glass) reflecting the high (L) in the low (K), or the macrocosm in the microcosm. In the word *like,* meaning both equivalency (this is like that) and admiration (I like you),† the highest principle (L) is coupled with the compressive principle (K) and equated: L=K.

In *lack* and *leak* there is a flaw: the L is not precisely equal to the K. There is a strange irregularity, or holy imperfection—an imperfection that vitalizes all of life and makes it possible for Loki to be his playfully mischievous self. (Cf. the grain of sand that, acting as irritant, provides the stimulation for the oyster to lay down the pearl.)

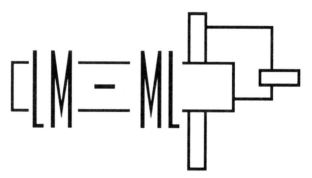

The *limiting* of the spirit (L) in manifestation (M) generates the word *lame*— of imperfect form. To *limn* is to draw, paint, or delineate. The *limitation* of life makes it possible to depict it, for without this limitation there would be no possibility of expression. (Consider the word *loom*—LM—the weaving of the robe of light (L) in the world (M). Thus *lumen, illuminate,* and

---

*Which generates Maya, the perfect stage for Loki!
†"I like you" also means equivalency: I admire you because I am *like* you. I am equal to you, or, as in Sufi love poems, I *am* you.

*lamp,* for light is generated by this closing-in (focusing), which creates the friction necessary to spark the fuel. In *loam* the clay-like earth represents the god asleep in substance. *Lump, lumber* (especially as verb), and *lummox* give a sense of the sluggishness of the Spirit, clad in the heavy materiality of this world. Consider, in this connection, the following words: *mill* (ML) and *meal* (cf. *molar*), the product of a mill. When one ponders, he weighs heavily, or *mulls.* A man can be as stubborn (resisting movement) as a *mule.* The noun *maul* (a very heavy hammer) is an excellent example, and so is *mail* (heavy armor). Somewhat different, but esoterically related, is *male,* the god-man descended and weighed down by an earth body. *Mile* (cf. *mille*) suggests a large (weighty) number. *Mela* (black) and *mal* (evil) refer to the opposite of light—that which has fallen. A *molech* is a consuming monster, and *Lamia* (LM) is a demon. *Lemures* are spirits of the dead weighed down by darkness. For this there is much cause for *lament.*

ML is not entirely heavy. Included are words like *mel-* (sweet or honey), as well as *mild, melody, milk, lamb, mellow, melt, mollify, moly* (magic protection against evil), *molt* (the casting off of a cover). Symbolically, the M provides the substance needed by the Spirit (L) to work its miracle of transmutation and convert lead into gold in the *mold* (which the spirit—L—is shaped—M—in manifestation). Living examples of this alchemical transformation are the *lamas* (LM) and *mullahs* (ML), teachers of the Way.*

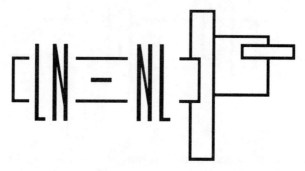

The N interiorizes or negates, while the L reaches toward heaven and dips down to hell (based on the principle that nothing can be raised up if it is

---

*Cf. *Islam* (and *Moslem*)—to resign one's being (IS) to that process that limits (LM) the Spirit in the material world. Therefore, "IS-LIM-ited" (cf. IS-LAME) or IS-LAM.

not firmly rooted). Since the L is everywhere, being at once up and down, and the N is nowhere, both letters are symbols of the Spirit and therefore tend, when paired, to reduce themselves to nothing. (In the Spirit, everything is gathered together, brought to an intense point of light, which burns to the core, baring essence.) Consider the words: *line, lane, lean,* and *lone*—all narrow words wending their way toward nothingness. Even *luna* (the moon) indicates reflected light and is relatively lifeless. (Consider the word *moon* backward—*no-om,* or "no life"—where *om* represents the sound of manifested life.)*

There are still more LN-NL words to consider, words that tend to bind, restrict, and narrow in an instinctive attempt to unify and reduce to nothing: *lanky* (tall and lean), *lento* (slow down, be still, be as nothing), *lenitive* (to lessen pain or distress—also *lenient*), *lens* (focusing light); *lien* (the binding of one's property); *loan* (from a root "to leave behind"—therefore, reduced); *niello* (from a root meaning black, dark, thus not visible), *nothing, nail, nil, null, knell* (mourning for the dead). The *Lenaia* (pertaining to the winepress) was a festival in honor of Dionysus, the god of the grape, which releases the wine of the spirit of the wine of Nothingness, ideally helping us to forget our state of separation. Lent,† the fast of forty days beginning on Ash Wednesday, is an aid for the soul's remembrance that All is Nothing (Ash)—LN.

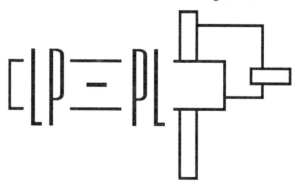

A key word in this configuration is *play,* the dance of life. P is thrust and activity, and L indicates the Spirit, rising and falling with the music. There

---

*Having moved toward Nothingness (NL), it is on its way back as the vehicle of new life. The moon needs our love (cf. *honeymoon*), and it is our love that reseeds it.
†The word *Lent* is related to *lenten* (spring). In the spring everything reappears out of the ashes of winter.

is the sense of fullness and intensity, a bubbling over. Thus the words *plenum, plenty, pleo-* (more), *poly, plethora, plural, plus, plush, plutocrat, plump, pulp* (pithy), *explosive, leap, lope, loop* (as in *loop the loop*—to make a vertical loop in the air), *pulse* (beating), *impel, ply, plucky.*

*Play,* as *lila,* is also a measure of emergence from the center (the P and L are pushing out, extending themselves). In the word *pelt,* we have the outer reaches of the organism, the boundary created by the body or skin. *Pale* also implies limits (the outer pale); its denotation *wan* suggests diffused color—extended, spread thin. A *pal* is an extension of oneself.

A *pall* is a cover (like a skin or a pelt), and to *peel* is to uncover the skin. A *pole* is an object characterized by extension, while a *peal* is a sudden noise or outburst that moves from the center outward. To *pull* is to move. A *pile* is not only a large amount but also a covering (outer reaches—from *pil*—hair (cf. *plume, pelage*), as in the *pile* of a carpet. *Paleo-* (ancient) is far removed from the center. *Place* is another key word in this configuration. It is the stage on which the lila, or play of life, is performed. The whole world, or any part therein, is a place, and the extent to which a man can dance depends on his perception of place—from the confinement of Prometheus to the mischievous rovings of the rascal god Loki. One thousand fairies can dance on a pinhead, or Shiva can dance alone on a corpse. For *place* (play-ce) is that divine movement of the Spirit, its extension into being, or existence.* (Actually, soul is the space of the spirit, its dwelling place.) To understand *place* is to understand *placid* (smooth). (Cf. *placate, please, placebo, plaster, pliable*), for *place* is existence itself, the need of the soul to be and to express its being.† And that gives it *pleasure,* lebensraum. Thus it is always worth taking the *plunge* (cf. *plunk, plop*) from istence to existence, for essentially it is a divine activity, the play of the gods, rather than a fall or *plunge* ‡ from grace.

---

*There are many PL words that have for their root "flat" (e.g., *plane, plain, placenta, plate, platy, please*). This is man's *place,* the space laid out for him, his royal carpet.

†To explode into a place—the "Big Bang" theory is applicable on more than one level.

‡*Plunge,* like *play,* connotes esoterically a motion outwards from the center.

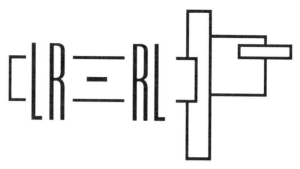

The usual understanding of *real* is the flowing out (R) of that life energy (L) from the center to the periphery so that it becomes manifest. From this frame of reference anything unmanifest is *unreal*. But under the aspect of eternity, the universe, as such, is real—manifest and unmanifest, the *ding and sich* and all its attributes (maya). Looking at RL from this perspective, the will (R) in and for itself is real* whether it be asleep or awake.

When RL is reversed (LR), one of the generated words is *lore*, which means

---

*What is unreal then, if the will is the all-encompassing Real? The question is unanswerable in our present mode. My intuition is that the will is not the finality, but is a subset of something not only unknown but possibly unknowable, which can be equated to the unreal. The closest we come to putting a word to it—other than such negatives as unreal and unmanifest—is to call it love, for to that Absolute (Love) even will is a handmaiden. The question may be asked: What do we really know if we don't know that Absolute (Love)? My feeling is that for all our science, poetry, art, and literature, we really know very little. To realize this profoundly is the beginning of wisdom. (I recall Rilke's moving lines: "Is it possible . . . that one has not yet seen, known and said anything real or important? Is it possible that one has had millenia of time to observe, reflect and note down, and that one has let those millenia slip away like a recess interval at school in which one eats one's sandwich and an apple?" (Rainer Maria Rilke, *The Notebooks of Malte Laurids Brigge,* New York: W. W. Norton & Company, Inc., 1949, p. 28, translated by M. D. Herter Norton.) Someone will argue: if we know nothing, how can we construct an atomic bomb? My answer is that we're arguing on different levels. Of course a termite knows something when it builds an elaborate house, and so on. But it's only a blind, instinctive striving, *as is the building of the atomic bomb,* compared with what man can know if he becomes identified (in the supreme sense of the word) with his source, the Absolute Love.

all that can be taught. Also, *law* (the approximate sound of LR) can be defined as the rules and regulations (the boundaries of the real) that guide our lives on earth. To *reel* is to experience a whirling sensation, which is an instinctive desire to bend back or return to one's source. (Cf. the serpent consuming its own tail.) *Roll* also conveys this circling motion, as if once a world begins to move it spirals around itself, ever seeking its source, in a reenactment of the primordial self-limiting of B (the activator of will* by circumscription, the creation of a womb that would nurture the seed of man). In *rally* (RL) there is a coming together—once more, the need to be at one. In *rule* there is the measure of maya, or the measure of existence—the extent of the will's (R) domain. A *ruler* (cf. *royal*) is *lord* (LR) over this domain. (Cf. *lar*, a household god, ruling over and guarding the domicile.) A *lure* (the desire to be) is what draws (R) the god (L) out of its center, while a *liar* is overextended, having lost touch with the center. (Cf. *roil, rile,* and *rail at*—the state of agitation resulting from this overextension, or even extension, of the will.) More peaceful than *roil* is a *rill* (rivulet), where the flow of water (the manifestation) is in harmony with the will. Similarly, a *rail* can move the mercavah (man as vehicle) peacefully along his destined track. The word *learn* is generated by the LR root, for it is the movement (R) of life (L) away from the center that provides the environment for learning. (Cf. the casting out from the Garden of Eden, which heralded the beginning of man's quest for knowledge.)

---

*Will* is related to *while* (a period of time), for without *will* (the movement into being) there is no time. Therefore "to *while* away the time" could also be rendered "to *will* away the time." Incidentally, *wile* as trick or artifice is also related to *will*, for without will there could be no *wile* (cf. *leer*—LR). Also, compare *while* (time) to *wile* (deceit), for only when time began was deceit possible.

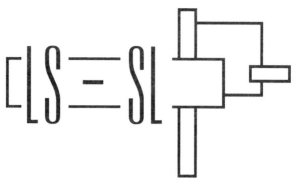

The life principle (L), reducing itself (cf. the Lurianic doctrine of Tsimtsum) by means of its own transformation powers (S), assumes the form of a *soul,* which can be defined as the reduction of spirit into a formalized expression. So lofty is this concept of reduction that it is reflected in many SL words. To *seal* is to close off, reduce access to. *Sole* is unique, reduced to one. Reduction is also found in *slay, lose, less, lease, louse* (reduced in size), *lass* (not fully grown), *sully* (to reduce the worth of), *lassitude* (reduction in strength), *leash* (curb, restrain), *list* (formerly a border), *lists* (fence of stakes), *lasso* (to reduce the intensity of, restrain with a noose), *slum* (impoverishment), *slumber* (reduced consciousness), *slump, slut* (lowlife), *seldom, self* (as in *soul*—enclosed, cut off, reduced), *solo, silent, seleno-* (moon—reduced or reflected light), *slack, slake, slander* (reduce worth), *slash* (reduce drastically, as in slashed prices), *slave* (bondage), *sloppy, sleazy, sluggish* (reduced activity), *slight, slim, slow, slip* (in one denotation, to lose strength), *slit* (cut off, severed), *sliver, slog* (move with great effort), *slop* (reduced to waste), *sloth, slouch, slough, solvent* (reduce the size of), *sell* (give up, let go, and in return become enriched), *sullen* (withdrawn, gloomy—reduced in spirit), *soil* (blemish, reduce the perfection of).

Reduction can also be positive. The Fall of man can become a degradation and a negation of his spirit, which leads to all the ills of the world, but this Fall can also be a planting, the burial of seed into the ground of being, out of which the resurrected man arises. Thus SL also generates *sal* (*salt,* the symbol of spirit, but also *salus* (health). *Sol* is sun, the fire of transmutation which bares essence. Spelled backwards, Sol becomes *los-e:* that fire is fueled by the giving up or *loss* of life. Consider in addition the following: *lust* (the desire for life), *lush, luster, salient, silk, silver.*

To walk the middle path between LS-SL is to be *sly*—to be one who knows what purpose the reduction serves. To be *silly* is to know how to be humble (reduce oneself in a spiritual way). A truly silly person exposes the innocence* of the divine fool.

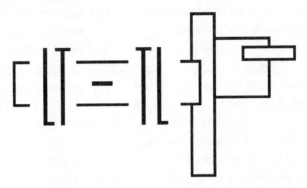

*Let* is the key word in this configuration, meaning permit, but also hinder (as in tennis parlance—a let ball). This holding back illustrates admirably the function of T as cross. Life (L) emerges from the growing point (the point of crossing over) and from there extends itself and grows *tall* (TL). But life is also hindered at the crossroads, for the path leading to transformation is beset with difficulties.

Extension words relating to TL-LT are *tail, tell* (relating a series of incidents), the many *tel* words (*telescope, telegraph, telephone, telepathy, teleology*—the study of final causes, ends, or purposes), *toll* (a charge for passing over a bridge or a designated distance, as in toll road), *litter*[†] (LT—the multiple births of an animal), *latitude* (extent, scope), a *lot* (many).

The resistance to this transformation is expressed in such words as *lute* (in one of its denotations a clayey cement, a sealing agent), *late* (delayed), *lout* (stupid, clumsy person), *latch* (fasten), *Lethe* (forgetfulness), *lethargy*, *-lite* (a combining form meaning "stone," as in *cryolite*), *loath, lotus* (forgetfulness, as in the lotus eaters).

As with every configuration, a sharp line cannot be drawn between opposites, for that which hinders also helps. Obstacles can make us grow stronger. Thus the *lute* (clay) that obscures our light and makes us forget

---

*Innocence or in-no-sense—that is, not *sullied* by the five senses or material world.
†Litter also refers to scattered waste material which clutters and stands in the way or holds back (cf. let as hinder).

(*Lethe, lotus*), provides the means for transformation, for without it there would be no cross (T), no meeting of time and eternity. So to each man is apportioned his *lot* in life. That is, through the magic of transformation he is awarded his place (space or enclosure) to live out his life. But for this he has to pay a *tol-l* (*lot* backwards). In order to extend himself, to grow, to reach his "end" (*tel, teleo*), he must pay this price (*toll*) in order to pass through the eye of a needle, the opening between time and eternity. What does pass through the eye of a needle is *light* (also meaning of *little*—LT—weight—small), a burst of life's energy.* This is the sought after *loot* or treasure—the sacred fire that Prometheus stole from the gods. It is man's lot.†

So it is with music, where the clayey lute is transformed into a stringed instrument whose measured intervals of sound are pleasing to the ear. But all music depends upon timing, and time itself is a measure of manifestation, a measure of clay (lute).

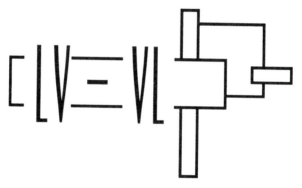

*Love* (LV) reversed is *evol,* the first four letters of *evolve.* Without love, evolution is unthinkable, for nothing can unfold without the imprint of love

---

*Consider the word *tilak* (TL), the red dot (intense point of energy) worn on the forehead of Hindu men and women and symbolizing the inner light or third eye. Consider also the word *teel,* the oil of the sesame seed. This was the real treasure the rock revealed when the magic phrase "Open Sesame" was uttered. It was teel—the buried light.

†Abram's nephew, *lot* (meaning veiled) lived in the Cities of the Plain. His veiling or covering was *lute*—clay, that is, his mortal coil. That was man's *lot*—to suffer this evil, this veil of Sodom and Gomorrah, which had to be fired by the *light* (LT) of the Spirit. In no way was it an evil *per se,* but a manifestation of salt or the

on its soul. The body of love is LV, the same as that for *leave,** which in one of its denotations means to give up, abandon, forsake. This is the essence of love: to be able to sacrifice, give up, and abandon the self for the sake of the other, or for the sake of God. LV is also the consonantal core of *live,* for love and live are essentially synonyms. Love sparks the will to live (e-vol)—the *vol-*itive faculty, for without love the will to live would assuredly weaken and gradually disappear. In love there is a crest, the apogee of human perfection, but the word *vale* (VL) is the trough, low point, or valley. The word *vile* (debased) represents the low point, where that which has been raised up (*love*) is being brought down (cf. *villain*).†

Lucifer, the prince of light, has fallen and his light has been extinguished.

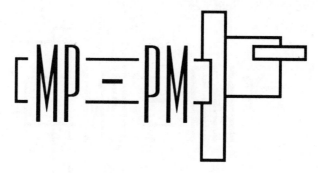

*Pome* (fruit) is a key word in this configuration. The P as power of the male to activate and the M as the power of the female to receive or to bring forth,

---

crystallized spirit (Lot's wife turned to salt). This is the stone (*litho*) in the LT configuration. But it is also the philosopher's stone in which slumbers the concealed light.

*Cf. *lave*—washed away, *leavings.* In this connection a leaf is that which is dropped from a tree, sacrificed in the fall as a life-preserving measure.

†Related to *villain* esoterically (but not etymologically) is *villus* (hair, that which covers). The moment man covers (cf. *veil*) himself with a self, shell (cf. egg or ego—essence protected by a shell), or suit of hair (cf. "and the first came out red, all over like a hairy garment; and they called his name Esau"—Gen. 25:25), at that very instant he became *vilified* or wrapped in a hairy cocoon preparatory to transformation. The French word *ville* (city, town) is related (esoterically only), for a city as opposed to the country, has lost its virginity. Traditionally speaking, it's a place where the *vile* hang out.

when conjoined generate the child, or fruit (pome—PM). This swelling (to be great with child) is reflected in *pomp, pimple, pompous, pompon, pommel, pumpkin, pimp* (fat with lust), and *pump* (inflate). Then there is *moppet,* a child (cf. *mop* as child—now obsolete). The prefix *pam* is an alternate form of *pan* (all), as in *pamphagous* (omnivorous). A *map,* child of M and P, is a representation of the creation or world.

The strong mutual attraction of P and M (active and receptive, male and female, positive and negative) generates such words as *pummel* (to pound), *pomace* (crushed fruit), *pumice* (volcanic rock), *pemmican* (dried meat pounded into a paste), *pom-pom* (rapid firing of a gun), *mop* (up)—defeat decisively. In *mope,* the clash of opposites (M and P) takes a destructive turn, and there is a letdown.*

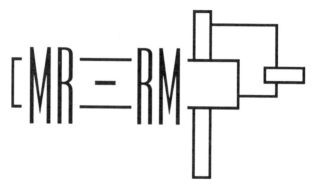

The key word in this configuration is *more* (MR). M, as water, is a reflecting medium, serving as nature's *mirror* (cf. *mare*—the sea). In water the subject becomes an object to be pondered. It is duplicated—becomes *more*. The R as will, moving into and back from the world (cf. *re*-flection) helps establish this subject–object relationship. The word *mire* (muddy ground) accents the complications arising from the involvement of life in *mare,* the waters of manifestation. *Mere,* meaning pure or only (a *mere* boy), reflects back the crystal-clear image of the sun (cf. *mirror*). It is that pris-

---

*To lift that gloom one need have only a vision of the reconciling force. Only then can mope be transmuted to mop—defeat decisively or make a clean sweep.

tine state of the still waters before they become muddied, *mired, marred,*\* *or murky.* Likewise with *morn* and *mourn:* one is light, reflecting the brightness of the day on the surface of the sea (*mare*), while the other is a response to the dark when the day is done (*mourn*).†

A *miracle,* then, is not any one specific occurrence but all of life, including the seemingly most prosaic events. You have feet—that's a miracle. But to be is an even greater miracle!‡

A *moor,* as swampy wasteland, is a mixture of *mare* and *mire. Mor* is a layer of humus (cf. *mortar*).

By means of this primordial reflection of images in maya, man learns how to perceive shape and form (cf. *morphic*), and in doing so he becomes identified (fixated upon) this image of himself in the water (as did Narcissus). Thus he becomes *immured* by it. To *marry* is to fall in love with the

---

\*The word *mar* (spoil, impair, damage) is an esoteric root of the word *marry.* Etymologically, marry stems from the Hebrew *môrâo* (*mem, aleph, waw, resh*), meaning splendor, brightness, a torch. Thus the Latin *maritus* and the French *mari* (husband)—the light of the woman. (Refer to Fabre d'Olivet, *op. cit.,* p. 246 of *The Cosmogony of Moses*). Therefore, etymologically, marriage is a light, for when the yin and yang, or the negative and positive, meet a light is generated—the sun or the Son of Man. The esoteric root, mar, complements this in a magnificent way, for marriage is the mar-I-age, when the light of the ego (or I) is eclipsed (spoiled, *marred*) in favor of the one. So in the etymological rendering the light goes on, and in the esoteric the light goes out. But, as has been said, the meanings enrich each other.

†The U (you), or that which is other-than-self, introduces death (*mourn*) to the human psyche; for once the psyche externalizes itself (Adam gives birth to Eve) it can witness its own death. Before that, life and death were one. Awareness, then, begins with I/Thou or You. Thus *mori* (death—cf. *murder*) is to see your reflection in the waters of life (cf. *mare/mori*). So man becomes *mortal* (cf. *merd*—that which, like the mortal coil, is discarded). Yet because of his mortality man can be *merry*; the word stems from a root meaning brief, lasting but a short time. It is life in this world, reflected life, the play of light and darkness, of life and death (*mori/merry*—MR). To be merry is to dance with Shiva on a corpse.

‡Miracle—mir-akl—mir-kl: The reflection (mir—mare) of the high (L) or first principle in the world (K—compressed).

image one sees in the world, and to realize, ultimately, that you are one with it.

Through *mirror* and *mare* life is reflected,* made more, and so extended. This is maya, or measured existence. RM words tend to move in this direction. Consider, for instance *rim* (edge, border), *roam, room* (enclosed space), *rampage, ram, ramble, rumble* (rolling sound), *rumpus, romp, ramify, rampart, ream* (enlarge, make more).

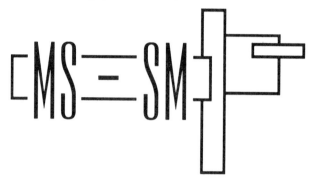

The M-S combination indicates the female, creative principle, for the S is the form multiplier (the tooth that tears) and M is the matrix or mother. S, as transmitter, is also involved in eating, nourishment (cf. the German *essen*), and general body maintenance. Thus the generation of the key SM word, *soma.*

Having established the basic concept of incarnation (creation of the body) one does not have to look afar to find corollaries. Consider the word *seem* (appearance), which relates to *soma* in a philosophical way; everything is not what it *seems* to be on the surface. Indeed, it may well be *semi,* only half of what it *seems* to be. Yet we suspect that the body (*soma*) and the soul are not really separate entities. The soma/soul division is *seminal* (SM), a splitting up that allows for the planting of the seed (*semen*).

The word *some* (cf. semi), in its most general sense, means "not all," which is to say that in *soma* something is *missing* (MS). This concept of missing is

---

*This reflection makes *rumination* (RM) possible, for to ruminate is to chew the cud, or turn back on the self (the reflecting object), to contemplate the still waters of the mind.

applicable to *mass* itself, which is more or less the same symbolically as *soma*. To celebrate *Mass* is to rejoice in the bread (*soma*) and wine (blood or Spirit), which hints that Mass* is more than just bread but also wine. In other words, this seeming paradox that *soma* is only half is contradicted in the celebration of Mass, where the Body (*mass* or matter) is suffused with the Spirit (wine). Thus, in essence, it is the *same* (SM), body and soul sharing a mysterious equivalency (cf. *meso*—MS—middle). Both add up to the All (cf. *sum*—SM).

*Seam* is the line of juncture, where halves (semi) are joined, and the *seamy* side of life is the dark, rough, material side. But there is a *smooth* side of life too, the proverbial other side of the coin.†

On the *soma* side of things, where the spirit is eclipsed and the light obscured, it is easy to see how the following SM words are generated: *smite, smother, smirch, smudge, smash, smack, smith, smelt, smut, smolder, smear, smog, smug, smooch* (carnal contact), *smuggle, small*. Many of these words are impacted or pressed together, which is characteristic of soma— that which has condensed into matter for the purpose of acting out or becoming a vehicle for the Spirit. Thus we have the MS words *miser, misery*, and the widely used prefix *mis-*‡ (wrong, bad, no, not, as in *misplace, misfire*), all expressing this archetypal idea of being identified with matter. To understand this dichotomy, which is in truth no dichotomy, is to *smile*,§ to recognize and transcend the duality. He *smelled* out the essence."

*Mystery, muse, mystic* suggest contemplation of the miracle of *Mass*.

---

*Cf. *mess*, a portion of food.

†The word *mise* (MS) means agreement, pact. Here the two sides of life become reconciled.

‡*Miso-* (hate), as in *misogynist*, implies complete identification with self.

§It is told that Buddha, in his most famous sermon, said nothing. He merely held up a flower. His disciples were nonplussed, all except one, who smiled. Tradition has it that the master's mantle was bestowed upon the disciple who smiled as the one worthy to carry on the teaching.

"The nose knows. To know is to be enlightened, but the core of the word k-no-w is darkness (no, negation). Out of darkness comes forth light. Dark/light—*semi/same*=knowledge.

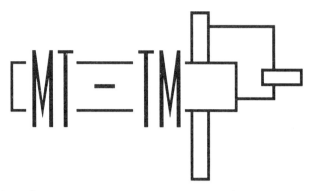

*Time* (TM) begins when man crosses over (T) into manifestation (M). In an esoteric sense, it is *emitted*.\*

Time is a function of awareness. It is a measure of the level of consciousness, and since there are countless levels of consciousness, there are countless times. Before awareness—the preconscious level—there is no time, and a full awareness—the superconscious level—time is transcended, for past, present, and future become the eternal now. *I Am That I Am* means that all identities are equated, not only in present time but also in past and future times. Full awareness brings a consciousness so quickened that the clock stops and we become what we are and are what we become—eternal beings that can divest or invest in time, at will. Therefore, there is no need to travel in a spaceship at the speed of light to experience this timelessness. One can do so (even in the Bronx) by raising the consciousness (quickening the tempo!)[†]

According to the Hindus, *tamas* (TM), one of the three gunas, is characterized by inertia. That is, when we fall into time (tamas!) we become inert and our consciousness slows down. But paradoxically, this investment in time makes it possible for us to transcend it. Investment, in other words, is a precondition for transcendence. Thus we have the word *tame* (domes-

---

\**Time* reversed reads *emit*.

[†]But not with drugs. Under strict supervision drugs can afford one a glimpse of his potential, but no more than that. Drugs are meant to be used as teaching devices only. Used in any other way they become self-defeating. How then does one realize that he is a timeless being? Only by enormous effort, which involves attitude, discipline, and love. The violin cannot be learned by popping a pill, and neither can life.

ticate). Taming is actually a timing process. In time we become cultivated, disciplined beings—individuals.

Food is digested in the *s-tom-ach* (cf. *tummy*—TM) and transformed. In time the entire man undergoes this digesting-transforming-taming process, which takes the raw material (man as food) and raises it up to a higher level of evolution.

Most other TM-MT constructions follow from this basic concept. Consider the *tom-tom* drums of Indian and African tribes, beating out (cf. the heartbeat)* the rhythm of life on earth. *Tom* is a word that has become associated with male (as in *tomcat*), for the male traditionally plays the more active role in the polarity, beating out the rhythm on his drum (tom-tom) to which the female dances. *Time* is also characterized by its activity (as opposed to the stillness of eternity), and thus can be symbolized by the male, he who plants the seed (as opposed to the female recipient). *Teem* suggests fullness, readiness to bear progeny. It indicates esoterically that time is pregnant, that through time we have the opportunity to give birth to ourselves. (Cf. *tumor*—to swell.)

A *temple* is the House of God, an appropriate formation, for when broken down into its constituent parts, *temple* reads temp-le, or *God* (Le, El, or L) in time (*temp*).

To *temper* is to mix in proper proportions (cf. *temperate*); that is, to live life rhythmically, to feel the pulse of one's existence. To measure time against eternity is to be in time but not of it. To be *timid,* on the other hand, is to lose the sense of timing, to withdraw from the activity of the world (cf. *timid* to *tamas*—inertia), to fear to participate in the dance. (As ever, the TM moves from the inactive *tamas* to the superactive *teeming.* It should never be forgotten that these configurations move along gradients.)

---

*The heart itself is our inner drum, marking time on earth. As the drumbeat is rhythmic, so our time is segmented, broken up into different notes. One of the most basic divisions of time, the second, is so called (esoterically, that is) because time is never primary. Like the second letter of the alphabet, B, its rhythmic beats are emitted from eternity, which like the letter A is before and after (two—second). To discover its center (now) is to discover eternity. *Tome* (volume) owes its origin to the concept of cutting off from a larger body of knowledge (cf. *microtome*). Time, too, is cut off—marked in divisions—reflecting man's fragmented consciousness and his abandonment to the world.

*Tomb* is time-bound and mute (MT)—utter silence. And since time is a measure we have the word *mete* (MT). But it is also a juncture, for manifestation is a wedding, a joining or interweaving of time and eternity. Thus the MT-TM words *meet* and *mate* (both meaning to join). *Meat* (MT) is also related to time, which is the fabric of our existence, the crossing over of time and eternity on the loom of life.* Fabric is matter, and *meat* is the garment of time, So in the words *mutt* and *mutate* there is a mixing of matters for the purpose of producing change. (Cf. the word *matter*—MT— itself as the fabric of time.)

The word *tempt* has an ancient heritage, originating as far back as the Garden of Eden, where Nachash, the Serpent, *tempted* Adam and Eve to eat of the fruit of the Tree of Knowledge of Good and Evil. To *tempt,* then, is to move into time, to become time-bound by our desires (temptations). But temptation is not evil *per se,* for to be tempted, in essence, is to make eternity audible—to make the stillness sound out (the beat of time). To be tempted is to want to dance with life.† It is to hear the tinkle of cowbells in the silent Alps.

In the beginning was the Word (Logos), which is synonymous with time. (MT-TM) generates *mot* (word—cf. *motto*). The word is a formulation uttered by the unspeakable void, and whatever is formed (sounded out) has a heart within it, which is none other than our internal clock.

*Mites* and *motes* (MT) are tiny particles, subdivisions of the Word related to the subdivisions of time itself. It is man fragmented (dismembered) in time. And so the command: Re-member thyself!

The word *atom* (a-tom, or without time) actually symbolizes a timeless unit that forms the basis of all matter.

*Might* (MT) stems from the concept that power can come only from reduction, confining (cf. *mite, mote*), for with that confinement grows the

---

*The sun (eternity) weaves its magic tapestry on the loom of night (time) until darkness yields up its thread to everlasting day. (That is, time realizes that its source is eternity.)

†"Lead us not into temptation" is a poor rendering of the esoteric teaching. It really should read, "Lead us not into the *trap* of being identified solely with temptation (the movement into time), but remind us always that we are centered in Eternity." For without temptation there could be no time and no world.

desire for release or liberation. The spectrum of life is caught up in the prison (cf. *prism*) of the world and will do everything in its power to break the bonds of the vessel* so it can be joined once more to its creator.

*Motive* (cf. desire, temptation) represents a moving toward. The basic concept of time is to move out of istence into existence, thereby generating the words *motion, motile,* and even *method* (the way of doing something, moving toward it). *Motif,* as main theme, is also a time word (MT-TM, for the essence of time is to focus (time as a cutting off or subdivision for the purpose of thinking (thing-ing) and analysis.†

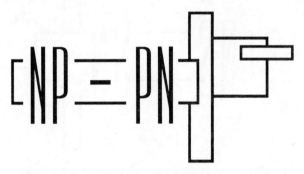

The N narrows, reduces, constricts, negates, and moves toward nothingness. In this configuration the P tends to reinforce the N: energizing it, drawing it out, and bringing it to a point of concentration.

*Nap* (short sleep) is the narrowing of perception. (In another sense *nap* refers to fine hairs.) If something is *nipped* in the bud it is caught before it can grow. A *nep* is a little knot in cotton fibers, a tying together.‡ *Nope* is no. *Nape* as the back of the neck conforms to the concept of narrowness.

---

*Cf. the "breaking of vessels" at the Jewish marriage ceremony. At that point the two are joined into one (when the imprisoned lights are released).

†The word *theme* itself is closely related to TM, for the TH can be considered as a compound letter. Therefore *theme* is very much like *motif.* Also, *mathematics* (MT) is the study of precise numerical relationships between the different segments of time and space.

‡Cf. *nuptials,* or tying the knot. This binding can reduce one's freedom, but as union (moving toward closer ties) it can enhance it. The ultimate tying together (knotting up) is to be utterly negated or notted—drawn out and reduced to "notness," or nothing.

This bringing to a point of concentration or narrowing down to a point is illustrated by the following NP-PN words: *pin, pen, pine* (needles, but also waste away, become as nothing), *pain* (feel the barb), *point, penis, poniard, pun* (quibble, fine point), *ponder* (point of concentration), *pang* (sharp and brief pain), *pinch; puny* (reducing to nothing), *pony, penny* (of little worth), *snip, snap, panic* (generated by the fear of being cut off or confined or by the threat of closing in*), *pent-up* is confined: *penned* in, tied, or knotted.

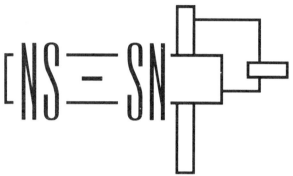

This configuration covers a broad spectrum. It is the Spirit (N) undergoing transformation (S) from *sun* (SN), its original splendor, to sin (SN), the darkness of manifestation, without light and subject to illusion. (Cf. *sine* and *sans.*)

The *nose* (NS—cf. *snout*—SN) is the measure of this process of breaking up—the son/sun is dismembered (cf. Osiris)—wherein the particles of the whole, each individual atom of it, are *sensed* (SN). Otherwise nothing could be *known* (cf. *nous,* mind, intellect, to *nose*), for there would be nothing (no thing) to be smelled out.

*Sin* is closely related esoterically to *sense,* which is to move outwards and

---

*Pan,* meaning all, is another example of the linguistic phenomenon "generation of the opposite." Just as the center or point is everywhere, the PN is a point that can expand to infinity. (Cf. the earth, as seen from the sun, as a point in space.) Likewise, in *open* there is the same generation of the opposite, but it is riddled with paradox, for to be open is to be focused on that narrow point of concentration—to *pinpoint* it! Consider the word *opine* (think) which is a focusing (tying together of thought to a fine point of concentration. *Punishment* (cf. *penitent*) is confinement. *Penis* can also be seen in this light, as binding us to our desires—the badge of Adam, his *penalty!*

touch that which is other than self. Adam sinned when he *sensed* the forbidden fruit. *Sin* is also related to *sound,* for to sound out is to sense. In eating the fruit, Adam sounded out his being, and an echo still reverberates in our hearts. By means of the *sun* man sees his outer splendor, the world about him, and by means of *sin* he experiences his inner splendor—good and evil—that which is taboo. In one sense it can be said that the Original Sin was to break up the Spirit, for in this way the Son is born as an intense concentration (or individuation) of light. *Sane* means essentially the same as *sound* (as in a sound mind). This movement into the world (SN) is a play of light and dark (good and evil) through which the senses are refined and the mind balanced (*saneness*).

Because man is heavily invested in manifestation, the weight of his sins bears down on him. Many SN words reflect this cutting off from the Spirit, his isolation (and all that follows from it) as an individuating particle: *snip* (cut), *snap* (break), *snarl* (confuse, tangle), *snipe* (as verb), *snippy and snappy* (sharp), *snitch, snatch, snub, snuff out, snob, snoop, sink* (fall), *snooze, sinister, snow* (as verb, deceive), *snare, sneer, sneak, snake* (deceitful person), *snook* (thumb the nose at).

Moses received the Law on Mount *Sinai;* the name is significant in the context under discussion because the law instructed the Jews in the art of transformation (SN-NS). To fulfil the Ten Commandments in the spirit intended is to transform oneself. It is a long way from the worship of the golden calf (*sin*) to the understanding of these principles (*sun*).

The cutting off and segmenting, or casting out from the Garden, precipitated time. And so the words *soon* and *since* (SN), both measures from the center or point of reference. A *sign* (SN) is a *signature* that represents or stands for something. The signature of SN on life is a way of stating that the name of the game is that all life can be seen as a sign of transformation. This is the *process* of life, but certainly not the *purpose* of it. The purpose we really do not know.*

In the prefix *syn-* (together, as in *synchronicity*), there is a hint that the process is reciprocal, that light and darkness are to be transcended, for in

---

*It is too easy to say that the purpose is to experience isness, the identity of the part with the whole, Nothingness, the Supreme Identity, etc. These are just signatures of *That.* I like to think of man as the unknowable Incarnate—whatever that means!

essence they are synchronous like the hands of a cosmic clock. This is the *song* of the Spirit that makes it holy and *sanctifies* it. (A *saint*—SN—is a person who can effect this kind of holy transformation.) The prefix *sen-*, meaning *old* (cf. *senior, senator, senile*), stems from the basic meaning of SN: stepping into the world, into time, and so becoming experienced in this interplay of forces. Only in this way can one become an elder, or the ancient one who has experienced this transformation.

To affix the suffix *-ness* to a word universalizes it (*goodness, wholeness, kindness*). To say "he is kind" is one thing, but to say "he is *kindness*" uplifts him immeasurably. The *ness* ending takes the word "out of this world," so to speak. The word is transformed to the very essence of what it signifies. It is the *ground* (cf. *nest*) from which the sun rises.

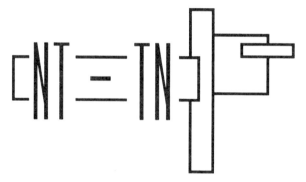

T as the eye of the needle, the point of emergence (in and out of manifestation), and the Spirit (N) together generate *ten,* the complete number, consisting of both the manifest (1) and the unmanifest (0). Since TN is a crossroad, there is a coming and going in peace. Life emerges (1) and life departs (0). TN is a font. *Net* (NT) is that which remains after the dross has been removed. It characterizes life at the source (cf. *nought*—) and sets the *tone* (TN) of our existence. The basic tone is the sound of the One crossing itself (inhaling and exhaling, receiving and letting go, using the dualities as a woven fabric that can be invested or divested), which strikes the fundamental *note*\* (NT—distinctive mark) of our existence.

---

\*The *not* (NT—cf. night) is negative or darkness (Source). The E, the silent activator, lights up the darkness. This strikes the fundamental *note* of our existence, its emergence.

*Nat* (cf. *nature, natal*), as birth, also moves into this manifestation, as does nut (seed substance). *Teeny, tiny, tinge* (TN), and *nit* (NT) hover around the zero point, while *not* becomes it. *Neat*, on the other hand, is newly emerged, well defined, clean-cut, sharp (cf. *natty*). *Noto-* (referring to the back, buttocks, support, as in *notochord*) characterizes NT-TN as the axis around which a creature moves.

TN generates holding words: *tenable, tenacious, tenant, tense, tendon* (from the Indo-European base *ten*—to hold taut). The emergent shoot holds on to and grasps (cf. *tendril*) a support in order to secure a foothold. It is the toughening process (cf. *tan*, TN, as in the *tanning* of leather) that roots us to our world. *Teen* not only refers to the years between thirteen and nineteen (often characterized by stress because a teen is neither here nor there, neither a child nor an adult) but also denotes injury or sorrow. This is a throwback to the emergence of man himself: born (NT, *natal*) into sorrow (death and time).

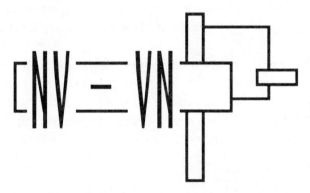

N as the Source (the dark substratum) and V as penetration, moving toward and joining to that Source, generate *nave*: central, hub (cf. *navel*). Likewise the appellation *von* (and the variant *van*) meaning from, refers to Source (von Braun is from Braun). *Nova* is new (cf. *novel*); *nevus* is a birthmark; *naive* is innocent (just born); *nival* is snowlike, pure; *novena* signifies (nine).*

*Never* (NV) is closely related to the above words, for to be renewed is to

---

*Nine, the number of birth also means new (cf. *nova*), for after nine the numbers "renew" themselves.

negate the self and be in touch with the Source, which is no-thing. Other VN words reinforce this: *vain* (empty), *vanquish* (reduce to nothing), *vanish*, *vane* (moved by the Spirit or the wind).

*Venus* (goddess of love) is generated by this configuration, for love is the source of our renewal. Love gives us birth. But to love is also to desire, and all that desire implies.* Thus we have the word *van,* as in *vanguard* (cf. adventure)—to be in front, in the foremost position. Consider also the word *vine* (moving forward, creeping ahead) and *vin†* (wine) as the product of the vine.

*Venal* and *vendor* can be traced back to the Latin *venus* (sale) and *venalis* (salable), which can be related to *Venus* esoterically. To sell, it is first necessary to arouse desire in the potential buyer—enough desire for him to sacrifice something he owns in exchange. Throughout history this ancient concept of selling (based on love—Venus) has been lost. For to sell, in essence, is to create the need in man to be willing to pay for the life he receives. This principle of exchange can easily degenerate into the idea of selling for profit, at the expense of the buyer, which was never intended in Spirit.

Another interesting VN word is *venery* (sexual desire, intercourse, hunting game, the chase). Both meanings stem from the same concept. Superficially, the woman is hunted and *vanquished* but the more profound desire, based on pure love, is to transcend (vanquish) the *animal* nature. Herein is the coincidence of opposites, wherein desire kills desire.

---

*It is *desire* that moves us into manifestation, tempting us to partake of the sacred, forbidden fruit. In this way we move ahead—VN, Van.

†*Vin* also refers to Source, as the wine symbolizes renewal through fermentation (death of the grape, and the release of the spirit). Thus the word *win* esoterically derives from *wine*.

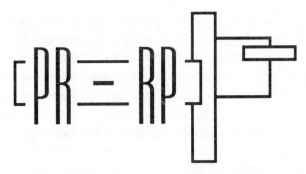

Emergence from the center or the will to grow (R), reinforced by the power of P (pushing, extending outward), generates the key word *ripe* (ready to burst with seed). The intensity of this will to manifest itself is expressed in the following words: *rip, rape, rap, rapacious, rapture, rupture, reap, press, prone, prick, probe, prod, prove, prey, pronto, pirate, peril.*

The combining form *pyro-* (fire, heat) expresses the intensity of the PR configuration. Fire *purifies* and *purges* (PR) to burn away the dross, and *purple*\* is a strong, vigorous color with royal overtones.

In the onomatopoetic *purring* (PR), the cat in its contentment reaches out (PR) and extends its being to you. *Poor,* in this connection, means *poured out,* overextended, and as a consequence diminished. To *pour* (PR) is to flow out, and to *pore* over something is to search intently or reach toward something. The prefix *pro-,* in one of its denotations, refers to moving forward or ahead of (as in *proceed, proclivity*); the prefix *pre-* usually means before in time or place, which extends the PR on the X-axis into the past (as in *precede, previous*); to *pray* is to move toward (PR) God, and *pride* is respect for one's accomplishments in the world, a measure of the extent to which man has activated his will to be. The ability to *prove* something also measures the power of the will. The prefix *per-,* in one denotation, means thoroughly, completely, very (*persuade, persist, perpetrate*), once more illustrating the intensity of PR, which in one sense is the will to love— to *per-fect* oneself. The prefix *para-* means extending beyond (as in *para-psychology* and *paradise*—above or beyond duality.†

---

\*Purple is the merging of heaven (blue) and earth (red). Therefore, the king, as master of heaven and earth, wears purple.

†The etymological rendering of paradise is a walled enclosure, from *peri,* around,

The Indo-European base for *par* is *per* (to sell or barter, hence make equal—cf. *parity*). Thus the word *par* has come to mean equal or common status, which is significant in the PR context. *Peer,* too, means equal. How does this relate to the concept of emergence from the center—the will to move out into the world? It is a way of saying that matter—the world (the circumference or *peri,**that which encloses, is somehow equal to the center. Thus the Tree of Knowledge of Good and Evil (that which produces the forbidden fruit) is placed in the center of Eden along with the Tree of Life. They are equal. It is as if the rays (R) of the sun are also the sun. Likewise *peer* (as verb) means to look out upon, but as noun it means equal.

The word *person* is derived from *persona,* a mask; *personality* has come to mean the masks we wear and the roles we play. However, the word person can also be rendered *per-son*—to sound (*son*) through (*per*). One definition actually complements the other: a person is someone who sounds through a mask. Now this very sounding out is the first expression of the Logos ("In the beginning was the Word") and this primordial utterance ("Let there be Light") activated the PR process, the process of creating universe, of personifying or individuating it. The mask (*persona*) through which the actor speaks is the *peri,* or circumference, which serves as a resonator. And so the word *experience* is generated—a venturing outward into the world (cf. *experiment*).† But experience also constitutes *peril* (peri-l or God, El, venturing out to the periphery). The peril is the experience of duality, of life and death.

---

and *daeza,* a wall. But esoterically it reads "above two" (from *para,* above or beyond, and *dise,* two). To achieve Paradise is surely to transcend the dualities! *Peri* is a Persian word meaning an elf or fairy descended from an evil angel barred from paradise until penance has been done. In other words, *peri* is man as circumference (*peri*—cf. *peripheral*) barred from his own center (paradise) until he purifies (PR) himself and realizes that the center and the circumference are one. So in a purification the dross of misunderstanding is burnt and only That remains (*par*—equal). Consider in this connection the word *part,* which means, esoterically, the whole also. (The *part* is on a *par* with it.) To *parse* is to subdivide, but it is only an exercise, a game to help us understand the whole. More than a subdivision, though, it is a focusing on the whole.
†And also *em-per-or,* he who rules the outer world.

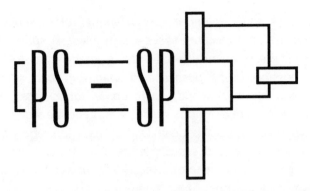

*Sap* (vital fluid) is a key word in this configuration. The P as male and the S as female (the multiplier of form, the possessor, the womb that transmutes) when conjoined generate the *sap* that energizes the Tree of Life (cf. *spa,* mineral spring). A *sop\** soaks up this vital fluid, which then gradually *seeps* (SP) out to nourish humankind.

The basic attraction of S and P to each other creates the word spirit (SP),†
in which they rest harmoniously. In *spiral* the S and P circle around each other creating worlds ("whirl-ds"cf. *spin,* SP). In *speech‡* they sound out, bestowing meaning upon the universe, and making it intelligible. *Spell* is an enchantment, identification, or involvement in the world or the Word (the different components that spell it out). To be under a *spell* is closely linked to the concept of the Fall of Man (cf. *spill*), where the father (P), the mother (S), and the god (L) are all asleep: S-P-L bound, or *spellbound!*

The life energy generated by the union of SP (sap) is illustrated by many

---

*Indeed, man is a *sop,* the bread (vehicle, material) of his life soaking up the wine of his spirit. He is, then, in the idealized form of Christ, that living *sap. Sap* also refers to the divine fool, drippy with the fluidic substance that he is barely able to conceal under the mask of personality. (Cf. the use of the word *drip* for a foolish person, which means in this instance, that he's leaky!) *Sap-ience* (wisdom) naturally flows from this.

†Pisci (fish), is the spiritual eye of the sea, (Cf. the fish as Christ.) Two other SP-PS spirit words are *pious* and *sophia.*

‡Cf. the *spokes* of a wheel, which connect the hub to the rim or the center to the circumference. The spoken word (Logos) does just that, for speech is that wedding of the S and P. The sound of unity is exemplified in OM. To speak, then, in the primordial sense of the word, is to utter sounds that draw out the center, extending them to the circumference (thus, esoterically, the *spoke* of a wheel).

SP-PS words: *spark, splendor, special, spunk, splash, spurt, spout, sprout, spy* (from the Latin *specere*—to see—as in *spyglass*), *sprint, spatter, spread, sperm, inspire, spray, pistil* (seed-bearing organ—cf. *pistol*—to shoot out), *piston, possible, pasha, push, spawn, span, spit, spate, space* (from a root meaning to flourish, expand), *spare, sprite, super, speed, spectrum* (radiant), *spleen* (seat of emotion), *split* (divide, generate—cf. *splay*).

But wherever life (*sap*) is, death (*sapro*)* casts its shadow and the following words are generated: *saprophyte* (feeding on dead matter), *sepia* (from a root meaning to cause to rot), *sepsis, seppuku* (suicide), *sepulcher, pus, piss* (waste), *spill, spoil, sopor* (sleep).

The energy of *sap* is opposed by the fixation or rigidity of death (*sapro*), as is illustrated by the following SP-PS words: *oppose* (hinder, stop), *pose* (stop, or fix one's *position,* as in *posing* for a picture), *peace* (the stillness that surpasses understanding), *piece* (singled out, fixed), *pause, position* (a fixed place), *posada* (an inn, where one stops to rest), *possess* (hold fast), *past* (that which is fixed), *post* (where someone is stationed).

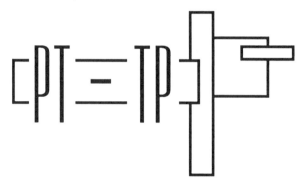

The concentration of power (P) at a crucial point (T) is the essence of PT, as in *peat* (potential heat), *Peter* (stone), *put* (move to a stated position), *pat* (fixed, immobile, to stand *pat*), *pit* (stone), *pet* (as verb, hug or press), *pate* (head), *pater* (father as symbol of power and authority), *putt* (strike), *pot* (as in *potential* and *potent*), *patch* (to strengthen a weak spot), *tip* and *top* as points of power, *tup* (the striking part of a pile driver; also a ram, the concentration of power being in the horns, *pith* (essence).

---

*In the combining form *sapro-* (from the Greek, meaning death), the difference between life (*sap*) and death, (*sapro*) is R, or the will. It is the willingness to die, to give up the old form, that makes life as we know it possible. So death is not something that just happens to us; we *will* it.

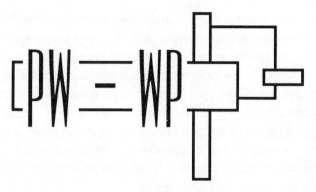

P, expressing power, coupled with W (which like the V is characterized by the impact or force of joining one U to another to create the concept of we, generates the interjection *pow* (echoing the sound of an explosion). Consider also the related words *power* and *paw* (foot as power base.) The word *pew* is also derived from foot). Then there are *weapon* (WP), *whip*, and *whoop*—a loud shout or noise. *Wipe* often suggests erasing, and to wipe out is to destroy or kill. (S-*wipe* is a hard blow. Cf. also s-*weep* and s-*woop*.) To *weep* is to experience the cleansing and soothing power of tears in an instinctive attempt to submerge oneself in the primordial sea, the waters of creation from which we all arose. Since water is the universal solvent, the hope is that it will dissolve (solve) all our problems.

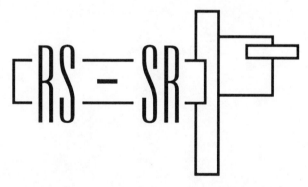

The will of the R, coupled with the transformative powers of the S, generates the words *rise, raise,* *rouse,* and *rose.* In reason (RS) there is the lift-

---

*The homonym *raze* (to tear down or destroy) means just the opposite! The transformation powers of S along with the will or R do not work solely in one direction. For a new house to be *raised* up, the old one must first be *razed.* (Cf. the story of Christ's crucifixion (*razing*) and the subsequent resurrection (*raising*). *Ruse*

ing, transcending power of thought. *Rustic* (from the Latin *rus,* "country," connotes wild, uncultivated growth. *Roose* is praise (to raise one up). A *rooster* by crowing at sunrise rouses one from slumber. A *roost* is a resting place. *Rest* is the midpoint on a continuum that begins with *raise* and ends with *raze;* neither growth nor destruction would be possible if there were no central point of rest. The will to transcend *rests* in that quiet place. In Latin, *res* means thing or object—anything real. In connection with RS, the will to transcend, it is to be understood in an esoteric sense: that hidden within every thing (*res*) is the desire to transcend or return to its source—to rise up again out of its limitation.

In the word *seer* (clairvoyant) the S burns through and the R reinforces it. Thus the *seer* * can see through an object by transcending it. Also, in saw (the sound of SR) there is this cutting through in terms of both vision and tool. *Sure* (cf. *certain*—SR-tain) also has the same implication: direct movement toward, and a burning through that assures. In *sour* the burning through is decomposition, and in *sore* the burning involves festering. Even *sorry,* in the sense of *sorrow,* means overwhelmed with pain or grief that bares the heart. The title *sir* (SR) lends dignity to a man's name, raises his status, makes him a *seer* (cf. *soar*). And, of course, to *sire* is to beget a child whose birth is the fruit of transcendence.

---

(as deception) moves toward *raze* (the breaking up of patterns). Likewise with *rash, rush, rascal, rasp,* and *rust.* The word *siren* (SR—seductive woman) is a cross between *raise* and *raze,* for not only can she *rouse* someone, but if he is not on his guard (centered in his resting—RS—point) she will surely *raze* him. The word *risk* is of special interest: rising (ris) through falling (k).

*Cf. *rishi* (RS) and *ras* (an Ethiopian prince).

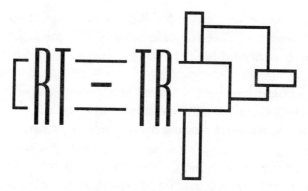

The key to this configuration is *tri-* (three), which is the will (R) to transcend (T) duality (the cross we bear). TR is also the root of *true,*\* which suggests that for something to be true there must be a coincidence of opposites that resolves the individual components (good and evil) and generates a synchronistic flash of identity. The trinity looms large in both Eastern and Western thought because it stands for the resolution of duality that is essential for humanity's preservation, for without this resolution we will fail to integrate all the diverse elements of our being and thereby fall short of our evolutionary potential.

For us this is a law; we are bound to it. (*Law* backwards is *wal-l*—enclosure, boundary.) For this divine light, Prometheus (meaning forethought, the light of the mind) was bound to a rock, or the principle of world formation, or the shrinkage of spirit into matter—*Tsimtsum.* Thus the words generated by this pairing will reflect the subtle shades of meaning of this experience of transformation. Consider, for example the trans (TR) words such as *transform, transit, transmute, transfigure, transfinite.* The basic meaning of *trans-* is cross over, go beyond, penetrate through. The root is TR—the will (R) to be as nothing (die on the cross) or the will to transcend (T).

This binding on the rock, which seems to be the opposite of transcen-

---

\*The word *true* esoterically means based on three, or nothing can be true which is less than three. The T is formed by vertical and horizontal lines (forces), and emerging from their meeting point is the R, the nascent will of man, his third force. *Truth,* then, is the realization of the three (TR) in relation to the one (TH), or individuating principle. Put otherwise, it is simply the realization that the three is one and the one is three. This is extremely difficult to see because man is "third force blind" (Gurdjieff).

dence, is also characteristic of this configuration. Consider the following TR-RT words: *transfixed* (impaled), *trampled, tread* (upon), *trammel, trial* (in the sense of hardship or suffering), *torture, trophy* (marking the defeat of an enemy), *tar* (tendency to bind or stick), *treacle* (molasses), *tardy, trap, trim* (cut short, cut down), *truncate, tear** (as verb), *terse, torso, turbid, torpor, starve, Tartarus* (Hell), *tribulation* (from *tribulum*, "to crush"), *triturate* (pulverize), *trickle* (a slowing down), *trick* (from late Latin, *tricare*—"to delay"), *travail* (original sense, to suffer in transit; *travel* can be traced to the same root idea), *tremble, terror, terra* (earth, the clay that binds), *tera-* (monster, as in *teratology*), *tire* (to weary), *attire* (cover oneself).

There are many more, all echoing the principle of TR-RT that eternity has become time-bound. It is fixed there and cannot escape except through death and resurrection.

The magnificent RT formation generates *rot*.[†] Consider also the root of *rotate*[‡] (from *rota*, wheel, circle around a fixed point). That is, to rot is to *return* (circle back, rotate) around that source from which we came. It is a self-feeding cycle, the universal serpent consuming itself. Reverse *rot* and it becomes *tor*, the root of *torrid* and *tropics* but also of *Torah* (the Law). The heat (tor—TR) of transmutation (rotting) burns off the shackles that bind the man.

This binding (cf. the Sanskrit *bindu*—dot or power point) is an inscribing, a laying down in stone. The laws of our existence are etched into the very substance of our beings, becoming the handwriting on the wall that we can all see but that only some can read. RT-TR words spell out in tablets of stone these commandments of the Law: *rut*[§] (groove, furrow, track),

---

*Cf. *rat* (RT), an obsolete word meaning tear (TR).

[†]Cf. the TR words *turd, trash,* and *tripe.*

[‡]Cf. *tire*, to weary but also as circle (a hoop of rubber or wood around a wheel). The coincidence of these concepts, to be weary and to rotate, is embodied in the Buddhist doctrine of *samsara*—the wheel of life we are so weary of. In this connection note that *tarot* is an anagram of *rotate*. Thus the deck of cards bearing that name is in truth a Wheel of Fortune.

[§]*Rut* also means be in heat (sexual excitement, cf. TR, *tor, torrid*), the intense desire to fuse the opposites, to melt them down, as it were, and dig in (cf. *rut* as furrow) for the sake of the child (the treasure of three arising out of the juncture of two). Note also, in this connection, the verb *root* (cheer for, get excited about). Also, the noun *root*, in its most general sense, is source, sun, or creative fire (TR-RT).

*route* (set path), *train, track, trek, traipse, tram, trail, trace* (path taken), *trol-ley, rite* (a fixed ritual), *ritual, rate* (a fixed amount, a set flow), *rat* (a Scottish word for track; also, an obsolete form of rot, a line of six soldiers), *rote* (fixed in a mechanical way), and *right* (RT—the right-hand path, fixed by tradition, flowing in channels, as opposed to the sinister or left-hand path, a devious or twisted one), *rotate* (move in a circular path), *tradition, trade* (originally a track or path), *term* (a fixed time), *trait, write* (RT) (inscribe in clay, make grooves, fix a line of thought). *Tree* is basic to our understanding; indeed, it is believed that the word *true* originates from it (firm as a tree). The tree is basically divided into three parts: the crown, the trunk, and the roots, and thus illustrates well the principle of TR-RT. In Paradise man had a choice to eat of the Tree of Polarity (good and evil) or the Tree of Life and therefore at the very outset was confronted with three (life in the middle with good and evil on either side). Christ realized the principle of three when he elected to be crucified on the Tree of Life, standing midway between the polarities, symbolized by the two thieves, both of which—good and evil—rob us of our potential.*

Perhaps the entire concept of RT-TR can be summed up in the word *try,* for the effort to overcome insuperable odds is built into the root itself—to *try* to realize the triple essence or truth of man, to *try* to do what Prometheus did, steal divine fire, the lightest element in the universe, light itself, which paradoxically becomes the heaviest once it is seized and incorporated by man.†

---

*It is indeed appropriate here to declare with Shakespeare, "a plague on both your houses!"

†To *try,* then, is to attempt to complete the triple sacrifice spoken of by Sophocles—the sacrifice of milk, wine, and honey. The sacrifice of milk is the sacrifice of the mother, or the body which nourishes us; the sacrifice of wine is the sacrifice of the soul, or that which activated the body; and the sacrifice of honey is the sacrifice of the child of the body and soul of man (cf. Abraham's sacrifice of Isaac), which is to say in truth that man in his most profound essence can be attached to nothing (Cf. Odysseus' secret name: Noman). This is indeed a most terrible trial for Man, and he can well lament with Christ (and for that matter, Job): "My God, My God, why hast thou forsaken me?" But it is his ultimate test, the touchstone of his truth, not to be attached to anything. Cf. Christ's utterance, "Do not touch me!" (Do not be attached to me!) Some say that this impossible task assigned to man is the root of his tragedy (TR).

The word *tragedy* itself may provide a clue: it means goat song. The goat is a

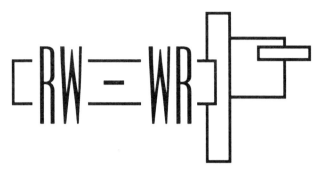

The sense of this configuration is best conveyed by referring to the Old English etymological root *wer*, man (as in *werewolf*). The Indo-European counterpart is *wiros*, from which we derive *virile* (referring to a strong man). Following from this, the basic sense of *world*, given some poetic license, is the home of man.

Why does the root *wer* spell out man? Think of it in terms of the *word—* Logos. Man (*wer*) is a creative utterance. Architecture has been called "frozen music," and man can be said to be a congealed or embodied sound. Since speech characterizes man, he can be likened to the *Word* (wer): "In the beginning was the Word, and the Word was with God, and the Word was God" (John 1:1).*

In terms of alphabetic analysis, the R is that sounding from the Center which rushes or roars throughout the universe. It is the will to be other than self. I am, but you *are* (R). To understand this function of R is to understand the nature of man, and the construction of the root that symbolizes him: *wer* (WR). It is that spirit that split off from itself to become man. That is his destiny. That is what man chose to do. Thus the word *weird* (WR) means

---

symbol of unbridled desire and obstinacy—the blinding desire to go at something without rhyme or reason. According to Buddha and to most people who think about it, this tendency of man (his goat song) is largely responsible for his tragedy. The scapegoat has become the personification of all our identifications. Symbolically, therefore, to do away with the scapegoat is to purify the man. Indeed, true, but the mote is in our own eye. We are the goats. And that is our goat song— tragedy.

*This, of course, identifies man (wer—Word) with God. Thou art That/ I Am That I Am. Jesus, as man, proclaimed: "I and my Father are one." God is inaccessible to us because Man is inaccessible to himself—"Man, know thyself" being an injunction largely ignored throughout history.

basically *fate* or *destiny*. Splitting (W) permits feedback or reflection, and thus *awareness* (to be *wary*—WR) develops, for by reflecting man learns how to think. Man is thus an instrument that sounds out (in his fullest potential) unity. The *Word* is his garment. He *wears* (WR) it. And just as a word can be defined as an instrument or vehicle that embodies meaning, so man as Word embodies meaning too, each individual man making up the complex alphabet of life—the infinite expressions of R-ness. But at the center of all these radiations is the I AM which makes of all men (the different spokes of the wheel or the different spokes of speech) One Man—the I Am That I Am.

To lose sight of this, to become disconnected from the Source, brings on a profound *weariness*. There is a clashing of wills and *war* is declared, a war fueled by the lack of realization that all the others (W's) are mirror images of the One. Instead of being a fulfillment of that ancient adage "know thyself," life becomes chaotic and self-destructive. This, of course, serves a larger purpose. The frazzled selves—all the alienated R's—are ground up into dust and eventually reembodied. But until that process becomes conscious the war will go on interminably, for the I Am slumbers. The real war is to slay the self that condemns other selves. The real war is to hate the hate—to see the mote in one's own eye.

War backwards reads *raw*, descriptive of that state of lack of cultivation that characterizes man. He is overextended. His R's are out on a limb. He has no aim. War is man (wer/war) in a state of unresolved conflicts, where one will seeks to dominate another at the expense of the whole. This schizophrenic behavior, characteristic of most men, is an ancient echo of that primordial splitting off of consciousness that made life possible. And this is man's dilemma: poised perennially on the razor's edge, he instinctively attempts to perpetuate that split even though he speaks in glowing terms of at-one-ment. The right hand literally doesn't know what the left hand is doing, both forgetting that between them "lieth the man."

The word *row*\* (RW), in its denotation argument, is easily derived from *war* itself. And so *warp* (R), twisted behavior.

---

\**Row* also designates a straight line. Compare this to *warp*. Both words stem from the same configuration: RW-WR. The meaning is clear in this coincidence of opposites, for to see the unity of man (*wer*), to see the connection between the double-you, is to see clearly (straight—row), but to lose that connection is to be

This constant clashing of wills generates *warmth* (WR)—the rot of dying selves is a seething caldron! But this is not to be misunderstood to mean that warmth can come only of negativity. A much greater warmth comes of the realization that the center is equal to the circumference, for the man is joined to the source of all light and heat and can direct the flow to himself in a conscious, creative way.

*Work,* in this connection, is that realization that the labor of man, his job, is to reestablish in his every effort that Original Seeing in which each alien will becomes articulated with his own. All *work* should move toward this end, whether it is the work of a lowly water carrier or the exalted work of the chief executive officer of a corporation.

The word *were*\* (including its subjunctive use) carries being out of the present into the past, thus drawing it away from the center, causing it to be subject to wear, weariness.

*Worm* (WR, original sense serpent or dragon) is the primal form that appeared to Adam and Eve in the Garden and tempted them to taste of the alien fruit and activate their will (R), to cut themselves off (be twisted). The worm in man is his own gastrointestinal tract, eating the apple at one end, digesting it, and spewing it forth at the other. Thus the worm, as man, is his desire to feed upon himself—to self-consume. (For what else is there to eat if all is That?) The appearance of the worm, however, is to lead man out of himself for the purpose of developing his will. But ultimately the "worm turns" back on itself, becoming kundalini, the serpent power, or the power to be.

---

*warped* (crooked). Man can master the third force and has the free will, in potential, to transcend. For nothing will ever be right for man unless he transcends. Until he makes that supreme effort, he will ever be at war with himself.

\*As *were* is drawn into the past, so is *wire* drawn out of (R) metal, with the capability of bending and twisting back (W) on itself.

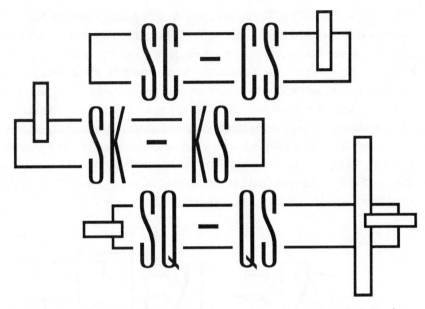

The KS pairing suggests burning (S) contact (compression—K), as in *kiss,* *cosy* (in touch), and *caustic* (rough contact). The word *cause* itself can be considered in this category, as the idea of contact is related to the idea of *cause.*

What follows are examples of related (burning contact) words: *scathe,* *scuff, scuffle, scrape, sclaff, scour, scourge, scratch, scrunch, screech, screw* (fasten tightly), *scrimp, sculpt, skate, skid, scrub, squeeze, scrouge,** squeak,* *squash, squelch, squinch, squish.*

The word *suck* (as in the baby's "burning contact" with the mother) and the word *sick* are related esoterically. For to be depleted (as in sickness) is instinctively to seek nourishment, to *suckle.*† To *seek* is to express the burning desire to make contact with a mystery, to *soak* oneself in it.

---

*Dickens probably chose the name *Scrooge* to depict his miserly old man in *A Christmas Carol* because he *scrouged*—crowded, squeezed, pressed his life into a miserable corner.

†Consider patient, as an example. Someone under a physician's care (a patient) would in all probability benefit immeasurably by learning how to contemplate his/ her life in a meditative way, i.e. learn how to be patient! For indeed, most of our illnesses, if not brought on solely by stress, are surely complicated by it.

The thrust or impact of this penetration (K) digs a hole (makes a hollow), as in *sky* (the inverted bowl or the mold out of which the moon and stars are born). Likewise, the *skin* is the envelope or container of the body. The terrible compression (K) or transmuting force needed for man to evolve is expressed philosophically in *sake* (motive, cause, reason). The suffering is "that for the sake of which." Or simply, it was for That, for His sake.*

The word *sacred* (SC) stems from hollowed out, hallowed, holy (cf. *sac, sack*), originating from man's burning desire to know himself, to penetrate (dig into) his nature, Thus the root word *scire*, "to know" (cf. *science, skill, scry, to divine*). The word *psyche* carries the SK sound for that part of the mind that seeks knowledge and understanding.

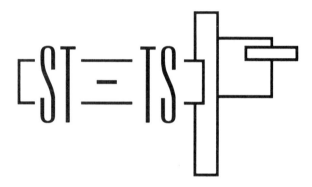

The T as the crossroads or meeting place between where new life emerges, and the S as the fire of transmutation, when conjoined generate *site*, the place where something *stands* (ST†). *Seat* refers to center or location, as in a *seat* of learning. The *site* or *seat*, as the point of emergence generates *style* (pointed instrument) and *stoma* (opening, mouth—cf. *stomach*).

Sito-,‡ a combining form (cf. *sitology*, the study of foods), points to food

---

*In Japan *sake* is an alcoholic beverage. It is this terrible suffering—this crushing of the "grape" (in this instance, rice!)—that gives us godlike insight or makes us forget, depending on how we use it.

†This configuration can be rendered hieroglyphically as the serpent entwined around the Tree of Life. The serpent power is the transmuting force (S) symbolized by the serpent's casting off an old skin. By crossing ourselves on the Tree (loom of life) we create the resurrection garment or the garment of light.

‡Compare *cyto* (cell), a basic living unit or growing point.

(that which nourishes) as arising from the growing point where time and eternity, male and female, active and receptive meet. In essence, food is third force! *Seti* (sharp, prickly, bristled, as in setiform), *stick* (as verb, to pierce or puncture, cf. stab), *stigma, stipple, sting, stitch* (as puncture), *stimulus, stake* (pointed stick), *study* (pointed concentration).

A *tissue* (TS) is an interwoven mass composed of matters that have "crossed" themselves. (Cf. *toss*, to mix lightly, and *tussah* (TS), silkworm, from the Sanskrit *tasara*, or shuttle. To *tease*, on the other hand, is to un-tangle—a coincidence of opposites.)*

As the *seat* of man's potential, the ST-TS pairing generates *Set*, the Egyptian god of evil. Evil, in its metaphysical sense, is that compulsion to live (evil reversed) that Adam and Eve experienced when tempted by the serpent (S) in the Garden. It is that desire to taste of manifested life with all its pitfalls. Thus *evil*, in this sense, is the *seat* (cf. Set) of becoming, of emerging into the world (cf. *satyr*—ST). But in a most paradoxical way Set is the deliverer† too, and is responsible for our spiritual salvation, for to pit good against evil generates light (cf. *satori*, ST, and Lucifer, light-bearer).

The further man descends‡ the more evil he is exposed to, and the more likely are his chances of being overwhelmed by maya. In short, man becomes *sotted* (ST).§ (Cf. *saturated*, filled to the gills, and *saturnine*, gloomy). He loses sight of his original splendor.

*Test* and *testis* are closely related to TS-ST, for the latter is the seed bearer, carrying the potential for a new birth (through the power point). A *test*, on the other hand, is a measure of the fundamental understanding of the prin-

---

*But it also means to create a tangle!

†Cf. *soter*, deliverer, as in *soteriology*. (Incidentally to *de-liver* is to take the liver or life away; thus, to be delivered is to die to oneself. This is what happened to Prometheus on the rock: he was delivered by that Great Bird or Spirit. A magnificent coincidence of opposites!)

‡Recall that *diabolo* means *throw across* the threshold of istence—existence—Set—ST. *Devil* is also the root of *develop*, to raise up.

§*Sot* (now obsolete) was once a little child, an innocent. One can become drunk by the weight of one's cross (cf. Sinbad's drunkenness when he bore the weight of the Old Man of the Sea on his back), but be an innocent—a lost soul. The ST-TS process can renew one or make drunk; most likely it will do both.

ciples embodied in the concept of TS-ST. To pass that test is to comprehend the mystery of the pivotless pivot. It is to *taste* (TS) of that essence, an elixir made only at the point where time meets eternity.

But since ST-TS is a threshold, a dweller guards it (cf. the Sphinx) and will not let us pass until we solve its famous riddle.* In other words, it is taboo to cross the threshold, just as it is taboo to eat of the Tree of Knowledge of Good and Evil. Many ST-TS words echo this ancient interdiction—from the absolute *stop* and *stay* (as in *staying* an execution) to the more heroic *struggle* and *strain*. Consider the following words, all of which indicate to some degree stoppage, constriction, cutting off, or slowing down: *stitch* (fasten), *stem* (as verb), *stasis, static, stat-* (a combining form meaning *stationary*), *stator* (a fixed part), *stricken, stalemate, stall* (as verb), *steno* (narrow, thin), *store* (let stand, not move), *strick, stumped, stub, step* (orphaned, cut off), *stereotype* (fixed), *stiff* (difficult to move), *still, stick* (fasten), *stifle, stingy* (holding back), *stint* (stop), s*tubborn, stow* (stop, as in *stow* the chatter), *stuffed* † (closed off, stopped up), *stultify, stolid, stupid, stunned, stupe* (medical compress), *sturdy* (unyielding—cf. *strong*), *sty* (to stop up, as pigs in a pen), *stone* (in the sense of thicken—resistant), *stymie, styptic, starve, stygian* (hell as binding), *strangle, strand* (bound together), *strap, strait* (confined), *suttee* (death, but also resurrection).

The Savior is transfixed to the cross—bound to it. But for him the crucifixion is a creative act of liberation in which he has found his true center. And so a *star* (ST) is born, the light paradoxically being generated by his density or the depth to which he descended (Lucifer as light-bearer).

---

*What goes on four feet in the morning, two feet in the afternoon, and three in the evening? The classical response is man, for in the morning of his life he crawls on all fours, and in the afternoon of his life he walks erect, but in the evening of his life he needs the assistance of a cane or a staff. The cane is a symbol of something much more essential. In the evening of his life, when man acquires wisdom and becomes a sage, he will walk on three: that is, all his polarities will be resolved and transcended. Only a man who understands the law of three and practices it in his life can overcome the Sphinx, which stops us on the crossroads of life and says, "Nay, do not enter here!" (cf. *sphincter*).

†*Stuff* is also raw material, essence: the *stuff* of which we are made. How easily it clogs the pipes!

Basically, the ST-TS is foundation, man's bottom line, and thus has a sta-
bilizing influence. This is reflected in the many ST-TS words that have as
their root some form of *stand,** that which we are based on—our understanding.

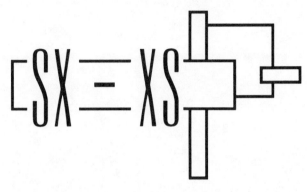

By the conjoining of S and X, the multiplier of forms (S) emerges through
the point (X) that marks the meeting of istence and existence. Thus through
*sex* the unknown X expresses itself in infinite forms (S). In the word *excess*
(XS), the multiplier (S) passes through the hole in space (X) dividing Nothingness from Being. In *exist* (XS), life in its myriad aspects (S) emerges from
the unknown (X) istence ("is tense" or present tense: now).

---

*For example, *stable, steady, station, stay* (*staying* power), *statue, stationary, state,*
etc.

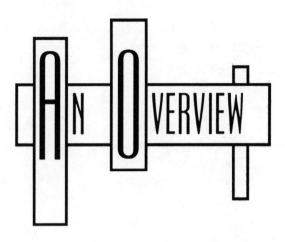

The alphabet can be arranged in such a way that the A pairs off with the Z and the M with the N:

| | | | | |
|---|---|---|---|---|
| A | 1 | A | Z | 26 |
| | 2 | B | Y | 25 |
| | 3 | C | X | 24 |
| E | 4 | D | W | 23 |
| | 5 | E | V | 22 |
| | 6 | F | U | 21 |
| I | 7 | G | T | 20 |
| | 8 | H | S | 19 |
| | 9 | I | R | 18 |
| O | 10 | J | Q | 17 |
| | 11 | K | P | 16 |
| | 12 | L | O | 15 |
| U | 13 | M | N | 14 |

The alphabet, as a whole, describes a progression from the Absolute Potential (A) to the Absolute Actualization (Z), the halfway mark being MN, or MAN.

Since the A and Z (potential and actual) complement each other, as do the M and the N (matter and spirit), it may be worthwhile to check out the other pairs in the chain:

| | | | |
|---|---|---|---|
| A | Potential power | Z | Actual power |
| B | Foundation of Life (the base) | Y | Affirmation of Life (the apogee) |
| C | Concentrated Light (that which can be seen) | X | The absence of Light (invisible, unknown) |
| D | Death or identification with matter (manifestation) | W | Life in manifestation (the realization of the other, that death and life are one) |
| E | Emergent Light (the breath of life) | V | The Lost Light the hollow—womb, world—in which that light burns) |
| F | Union, the joiner (restorative force that reunites) | U | The other, standing alone (separation) |
| G* | Organic transformation | T | The emergence of the new self |
| H | The temenos or sacred enclosure (house of the unicorn) | S | The sacred work of transformation carried on within this enclosure (the horn of the unicorn is the shin or tooth) |
| I | The individualized Light generated in the holy garden (sacred enclosure) | R | The irradiation of the Light as will, which cannot be experienced without an I to affirm it. |

*The GT combination is the middle pair of the chain. The suggestion is that GT does for the consonants what I does for the vowels. (Indeed, if the vowels are spaced out evenly with the chain the I lines up with the GT.) In the word *gut* (GT) there is an exchange between inner and outer. A *gate* is that which regulates movement back and forth across a threshold. Even a *goat* (GT), like a gut, is characterized by its ability to process coarse food. Thus, as scapegoat it receives our coarseness and is blamed for it.

J   The pent-up Light, locked
    up in manifestation

Q   The spark of intuition
    generated by the
    locked-up J

K   Compression (pressing
    together); the buried seed

P   Extension, pushing out
    and unfolding of the
    shoot, generated by the
    compression of K

L   That which rises and falls as a
    function of breathing

O   The realization that
    heaven and hell are
    reciprocal functions,
    an integral part of
    breathing

M   Matter

N   Spirit

Another way to view the alphabet, based on the ineffableness of A and Z, is to separate the first and last letters and divide the remaining twenty-four into groups of three:

| POTENTIAL | A | 1 | | 01 | |
|---|---|---|---|---|---|
| Life | B | 2 | | | |
| Awareness | C | 3 | 9 | 1 | |
| Death | D | 4 | | | |
| Light | E | 5 | | | |
| Sex | F | 6 | 18 | 2 | |
| Dark | G | 7 | | | |
| Enclosure | H | 8 | | | |
| Individuation | I | 9 | 27 | 3 | |
| The pent-up I | J | 10 | | | |
| Hardness | K | 11 | | | |
| Pulsation, growth | L | 12 | 36 | 4 | |
| Softness | M | 13 | | | |
| Negative | N | 14 | | | |
| Neutral | O | 15 | 45 | 5 | |
| Positive | P | 16 | | | |

| | | | | |
|---|---|---|---|---|
| Hidden | Q | 17 | | |
| Will | R | 18 | 54 | 6 |
| Revealed | S | 19 | | |
| Transcendence (raising up) | T | 20 | | |
| The World | U | 21 | 63 | 7 |
| Penetration (digging down) | V | 22 | | |
| Division, denial (the split between I and Thou) | W | 23 | | |
| Revelation (Christ) | X | 24 | 72 | 8 |
| Union, affirmation | Y | 25 | | |
| ACTUALIZATION | Z | 26 | | 10 |

The total of each group of three is divisible by nine. (The A and Z together are also divisible.) There are eight groups and two ineffables, like the ten sephiroth of the Qabbalah. The A and Z form a separate category similar to the two ineffables, Kether (A) and Malkuth (Z). The other eight sephiroth are Chockmah, Binah, Geburh, Chesed, Tiphareth, Hod, Netzach, and Yesod.

It is of interest that the "sum of 26" is also nine. That is, the numbers contained within 26 (25, 24, 23, 22, etc.) when totaled add up to 351 or, 9 (3+5+1). Since the alphabet can be arranged in a circle, the A linking with the Z (the "necklace" of God) it would be elegant if the sum added up to 360 (the number of degrees in a circle). The 351 falls short by nine (cf. the "casting out of nine"). Now the ninth letter of the English alphabet is the I, which man is missing; that is, he has no permanent I.*

One can see the whole alphabet as a play of three, with groups of opposing forces revealing a third. Thus the B and D reveal the C, the E and G

---

*Note also the Masonic symbol of the pyramid with the split-off eye, which can serve a dual function: either as an over-seeing eye (I) or as a divided one.

reveal the F, and so on. The middle letter in each group is nothing more than another form of the A, which ultimately metamorphoses into the Z.

Thus awareness (C, to see) is made possible through the opposition of Life (B, being) and Death (D). Sex (F, or joining) is the wedding of Light (E, the window) and dark (G, the interior workings of the gut). That is, the Principle of Darkness is impregnated by the Principle of Light, and the Son of Man is born. The I (an individualized form of the A) is revealed, or individuation is made possible, by the I's confinement (the pent-up I or J) to a self (H). Hardness (K) and softness (water or M) intermingling make life (growth, pulsation, timing) possible, as in the angular male and circular female, and the compressed seed and the soft earth that receives it. The play of negative (N) and positive (P) reveals the neutral (O), or the neutral generates the negative and positive. By the play of the hidden and the revealed (Q the hidden intuitive and S the multiplier or revealer of form), the Will (R) is developed, for when the Soul (Beauty) is hidden it arouses the desire or will of the prince to seek her out and reveal her. That which is other than I (the U or world) is born of a wedding of the highest (T) and the lowest (V). It is a falling of the Spirit into its own Profundity. The Unknown (X, Christ) can be revealed in Man only through resolution of the opposition between Yea (Y, union, affirmation) and Nay (W, division, and thus, by extension, denial).

In summary, the three Mother Letters—A, M, N—are all that the alphabet really needs to express itself in broad, general strokes: the M "for all that God hath made," the N for all that is "unmade," and the A, as First Principle, to join them. Thus *MAN* is the Word of God, balancing not only the alphabet but also Heaven and Hell.

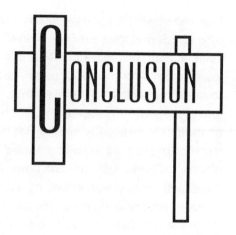

# CONCLUSION

The absolute A, which for all practical purposes is unknowable, weaves for Itself out of its own ineffable light a garment of Being (B), and by so doing reveals itself (C—as concentrated light) to Itself. This revelation is at once an intense brightness but also (paradoxically) a "re-veiling" or cutting-off (D) itself from itself—the creation of a world out of the void. But still the light of the universal splendor inheres in its creation, emerging (E) as the myriad suns that light up the heavens, all of them in essence joined (F) to that central sun (the absolute A). In G there is the replication of the primal movement of self-enclosure that creates an organ system within the body of the grand man. In H this process of walling off proceeds even further until the indwelling spirit becomes confined to a self. However, the light of the absolute emerges once more as a faint glimmer in the individual I, which becomes the center or yolk of the self. This sense of confinement can be compared to Prometheus' being bound to a rock. Indeed, such is the suffering of the hero that his I is literally turned inwards (J) because of the intense pressures of manifested life. But this constitutes the molding (K) of the Spirit, the creation of a hollow, a niche for oneself that will harbor the light.

Once inside that hollow, a heart develops and the spirit experiences the renewed pulsations of life (L), its gentle rising and falling. And so the circulation of this current is assured. The waters of manifestation (M) wash over and engulf the spirit (N), both merging to create a vehicle for the man who stands midpoint between heaven and hell, good and evil, God and devil, and all the other polarities. In man, the spirit has descended to its lowest point—its moon, or nadir—and is now bent on returning to its source. From A to M all is involution. From N to Z it is evolution, the return of the soul to its source. In O Man realizes that the cycle bends back on itself, that essentially nothing has been lost, for the Spirit is always intact though seeming to be fragmented. In P the flower of man swells into bloom, radiating out in all directions. The Q provides the dark ground for this growth, the fertile, creative mind of man that nourishes the seed. T goes hand-in-hand with P and Q, for the three letters function as one unit, R being the will that ever seeks to find its way back to the Source. It is the will that animates the P, the will that makes it bloom. Indeed, it is the will that planted it in the womb of the mind to begin with. S is the enzyme that triggers the power of transformation, operative on every level throughout the whole of creation. Essential to the alchemical process, it assures man that all the scattered elements of his being serve as food for the self-consuming serpent. The T is the realization that no matter what transpires, life will emerge renewed at the crossroads, that every isolated U will be reunited by the process of inner probing; for by digging in and penetrating (V), man will uncover the roots that connect him to his fellow human beings (the W), thereby realizing that what he sees reflected in the world is but a mirror image of his own I. This realization solves the equation of identity for man, thus revealing the nature of the unknown X, which is equal to every other letter of the alphabet. This understanding is the highest affirmation(Y) of life. For to experience completely the identity of I and Thou, that I and Thou, that I and my Father are one, is to rise to the sphere of Z, which is none other than the Grand Aleph or the actualization of A.

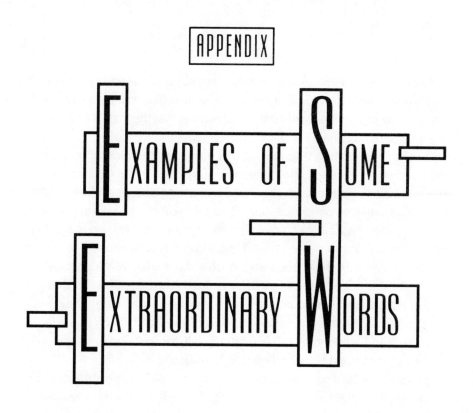

# Examples of Some Extraordinary Words

In addition to the meaning of the letters per se, words reveal themselves in a variety of ways to those who have an ear to listen and an eye to see. For instance, the word *extraordinary,* besides meaning *unique,* can also be rendered *extra* ordinary. That is, a man who is selfless and has given up pretense becomes *extra* ordinary, and therefore, fundamentally (and paradoxically), extraordinary!

Words are often lambent, playfully flitting about, as in *embarrass,* which can easily be rendered "I'm-bare-assed." When the word *cannibal* comes to mind I cannot but help think of the derivation my old teacher, Morris Frank, worked out. Since Cain committed the first murder and the ground consumed his brother, Abel, the collective unconscious coined the word *Cainabel,* which ultimately became its modern counterpart! The word *union* can be rendered "no-i-on" (*no* or *not* substituting for *un,* as in *un-*fit). This is a precise definition of *union,* for there can be no unity—union cannot take place—if there is an I (ego) on! The light of the ego must be extinguished for union to become possible.

The word *lesson* implies that a truly learned person is empty of conceit and has less on. Before God one must stand naked! Consider the interesting word *moron*, the playful connotation being that the man is now carrying too much baggage!

That life and death are so intimately connected can readily be seen in the word *child* (the energetic expression of a new life). But CH can also be pronounced K, as in *Christ, character,* and *chromatic.* Therefore, a phonetic alternative to *child* can sound like *kild* (*killed*). Likewise, consider *morning* (the new day) and *mourning* (paying one's last respect to the day, or the light, that has passed away). And think of *slaughter* (kill), which conceals within itself the word *laughter;* for to die creatively (consciously) is to release life, and this can give rise to laughter: the realization that life and death are the obverse and reverse sides of the same coin. *The joke is on you!* Consider the phonetic rendition of the word *laugh* itself (*laff*). Reverse it and it becomes *fal, fall,* or *fail*—all "down"words, as opposed to the rising sun and bursting bright light of laughter.

These words (and so many more) contain their own opposites, for to be whole at all implies the self-containment of the left *and* the right, good *and* evil, right *and* wrong, life *and* death. No matter how short you cut, the stick has two ends.

The word *individual* illustrates the point well, for an individual stands out as a unique and separate being. Yet, built into the word itself is the concept of the undivided (all one), indivisible in-dividual! The same is true of the word *alone*—separate, by oneself. Yet it also means all one—united. Actually, to be separate is a paradox itself, for when one is wholly separated (that is, divested from all there is), he becomes the All. Herein is the individual equated to the indivisible: the part equals the whole.

No wonder we have such trouble communicating! Nearly every word in the language generates its opposite, and so we draw our lines based on our experience of duality.* What we fail to understand is the principle of three (thesis, antithesis, and synthesis). Erroneously, we are led to believe by the evidence of our senses that one or the other is right, and in this respect we fail to communicate with our deeper Self or the truth of our own being.

---

*Consider even the word *I*; it can refer to the Master Self or the lesser self (ego).

In order to do away with this dualism we seek a partner, or *marry*. The word *marriage* actually means (esoterically) the mar-i-age; that is, you cannot behold the beloved unless his I (ego) is extinguished. I am thee, my love!

When one is *blessed* in marriage, the hymen is ruptured and blood actually flows. The word *bless* owes its origin to *blood,* for a sacrifice has been made; the I has been pierced.*

The word *moon* reversed reads *no om,* or no life (om being the sound of life). The earth is alive, while the moon is dead—but only apparently so, for the earth and moon form one entity. The moon, by the sacrifice of its life, makes it possible for the earth to live. During their honeymoon, newlyweds pay tribute to this mystery by depositing their seed so that this Great Being may be revitalized.†

The word *coincide* takes on a different meaning when viewed from this perspective, for to coincide in this respect really means to be together with (co) on the inside—*co-inside!* All life, when you come down to it, actually coincides (is synchronistic). for there is really nothing separate, nothing on the outside. Thus what happens, happens together on the inside: it *coincides!*

Thus crucifixion on the *cross* coincides with resurrection (c-*ros*-s). And the name *Christ,* although at once implying existential crisis, contains within itself the means of overcoming it, of "rising" (Ch-*ris*-t). Life can never be fully separated from death.

Man ever seeks to rise above the limitations set upon him by the dimensions that circumscribe his life. The fourth, fifth, and sixth dimensions, and even dimensions beyond them, appeal to man's imagination as means of escaping from bondage to space-time. The word *dimension* itself playfully suggest the way out of this dilemma, whispering to our inner ear that in order to move into other dimensions we must first die to this one; but because men shun dying (die-men-shun), their entry to higher worlds or other dimensions is blocked. It is the fear of stepping over into another world,

---

*Note also that the wise man Teiresias, like Justice, is blind. The eye (I) has been pierced.
†The cow in the nursery rhyme, by jumping over the moon, also delivers nourishing milk to resurrect this dead entity.

of falling off the edge of the earth into a bottomless abyss, that bars the way.

The antagonism (rather than the reconciliation) of I and Thou is expressed vividly in the word *enemy*, which can be rendered playfully *NME*, or *not mine or me*. Simply—*not me*. An enemy is anything out there that threatens the me or the my. Instinctively, in order to balance our natures, we (unconsciously) project our enemies to function paradoxically as a means of separating ourselves from attachments. It is the wise person who blesses an enemy (turns the other cheek), declaring that what can be taken away was never owned in the first place. It is the enemy (end of me) that bares essence.

The *mother* embodies within her womb the world of the other, and so her name—*m-other*. She is at once the nearest, the dearest, the most enveloping and all-embracing, and yet that which is distant is not excluded, that which is other is incorporated into her soul. It is the same with the word *there*, which seemingly points away. Yet hidden within the word is *here* (t-here); for to behold the Spirit here *and* there is to behold the extent and breadth of one Being. Consider the word *father*, which closely resembles (in sound) *farther*—that which moves away and is distant. For the father, like the farmer, stands off. He plants the seed while the mother (or earth) embraces it. But still, like the mother who incorporates the other (she is both "farther" and mother to the child!), the father also contains within himself the makings of the mother: he is a *fat-her*. Buried within the yang is the seed of the yin, and vice versa. Man is the barren woman and woman is the fertile man!

Our language abounds in these paradoxes because as the Logos (the Word) it is the Holy Ghost expressing Itself as only it can in this dimension—through a polarity.* Meaning is projected, and if it is to be balanced must be seen under the aspect of eternity. It is a difficult assignment for mortals. Yet it is all around us. There is no hope of return unless we begin to understand this paradox.

To *cleave* is to split asunder but also to *cling*. "In my own way" implies freedom, but it also means blockage: that there is no one out there to stop me except myself. (I fear that I am standing *in my own way!*)

---

*As one among countless examples, to be "fit as a fiddle" implies balance, while "to take a fit" implies just the opposite.

To *forget* is to let go of something, to let it slip out of memory. But this is essential, for it can be rendered "for-get" (for-the-getting). To let go is the first step to being refilled or fulfilled.

The word *give,* etymologically, can be traced back to grasp or take. And a *gift* is akin to the Germanic *gift,* meaning poison! In other words, the supreme gift (according to the wisdom of language) is to "poison" the self and die to it.* Nothing can be given away unless it is first owned. A person cannot become selfless until he or she first possesses a self. Give and take, then are but twin aspects of the life blood or the electrical current circulating within us.

The *guru,* as embodiment of teacher, often stands alone as the other, someone the disciple can look up to. But playfully rendered, the word becomes "Gee you are you" (*G-U-R-U!*),† which brings back to the disciple the full realization of what it means to be YOU. Stated somewhat differently, it equates the two you's: Thou Art That and I Am That I Am!

In German, *gut* means good, which is appropriate esoterically, for the gut is the transformer, wherein that which is coarse is digested and thereby nourishes the body. This is *good*—very good! It has been said that "To the pure all things are pure," so that so-called evil, when digested by the gut of a wise man or sage, is transmuted to its Original Nature, that which is *good*.

And so man's *joy* is to *joy-n* (*join*) with his Creator, to *atone* for his sins and be at one with him. To realize this truth fully is to *know* (k-now) that man is an eternal ever-present Being, encompassing the past and future and living in the NOW. This is k-*now*-ledge supreme, the Absolute's *gift* or *present* to Man, "By His Presence shall He be *known!*"

This is the *law* of our life, that we are timeless beings timebound in a space vehicle that is subject to mortality. Backwards, the word *law* becomes "wal" (wall) or that which encloses—a limitation. The word *bar* (that which restrains) has also come to mean *law*. All law is based on limitations; indeed, the word *limn* means to make light.

---

*Recall the Shirt of Nessus, or the gift of poison, which by clinging to Hercules killed him. Yet it was this release from the mortal coil (of self) that restored his godhood.

†I believe that this rendition of G-U-R-U is old Firesign Theater material.

Man, like the unicorn, is imprisoned in a temenos, but is also endowed with that single horn (symbolizing his unified will) that provides the means of escape. The temenos is also the screen of our manifestation, the canvas on which we create and enact the drama of our lives. (If the stretch were infinite and there were no frame or focus for our minds, what possibly could be created?) To *know* anything is to have the freedom to cut off, to deny, to say "No!" (k-no-w). It is the magic of chiaroscuro, the shading of light and darkness, which brings out and adds to the depth of our lives.

So it is best always to remember that the word *let* at once means *permit* but also *hinder*. Between these concepts we live our lives. It is the razor's edge of being. Constituting the very warp and woof of our lives, it can be considered the *myth* that has created us. *Myth* can be rendered M-TH—the saga of the below (M, or matter) and the above (TH, or God). How the polarity intermingles creates our myths. Likewise with *math:* for how God (TH) and matter (M) intermingles creates our number system—our math.

Our words are miraculous! Think of the simple word *olive* and the magic of its precious oil. It cries out to us, "*O LIVE!* Sense the joy of life and be at peace with thyself!" And so as human beings, we all have the olive branch extended to us.

Man *owns* nothing, yet it is all his anyway. Whatever we think we own we actually owe. Even etymologically the two words (owe and own) are related: what you own, you also owe. It must be paid back. But first you must grasp it, possess it, digest it, and then only can you give it back as fertilizer for the new seed. So what a man owns becomes an obligation which he must fulfill by giving it up. And this is the essence of teaching—to pass on, in a form that can be digested, that which has been received.

Surely this is what the ancient injunction "Remember thyself" meant: to gather together the scattered parts of that Being. It happened to the Absolute as it happened to Osiris, for he also was dismembered. Ab means father (as in Abraham and abbot) and *solute* is that which is dissolved. Thus the *Absolute* is that principle of unity (Osiris, God) that has been scattered or dissolved in the world. Since it has been dismembered, the problem presented to man is to re-member it, and *solving* this problem simply means that man must bring it out of *solution*—rescue it from submersion in the waters of life. It is *Noah* (cf. *knower*) coming to rest above the flood level.

To understand this mystery of submersion, dissolution, and resurrection

is to sit on the *throne* of the Lord Absolute. Esoterically, the word is a contraction of the numbers three and one (thr-ee-one, or throne), for to understand the tri-unity entitles one to a seat on the exalted throne. The trap
is not to see the whole (the three-in-one or the *throne*) and to become en-
tangled in the part (*trap* backwards)! The *treasure,* however, is to be able
to behold the three lights, which esoterically the word *treasure* means
(treas-ur).* This constitutes the basic *understanding* (to stand under, the infrastructure or that which supports us) of man.

One of the most playful of words is *wisdom.* It sounds very much like
the compound wise-dumb; for to be wise is always to incorporate within
one's being the goof or the ignoramous, as one is never separate from it.
Only a wise man in his wisdom knows this. That is why Christ *chose* to be
crucified between two thieves, for in his wisdom he understood the principle that the clay can never be held apart, and that which robs us of our
heritage must be embraced and loved (the Judas kiss) so that its light can
also be restored. And this is the *wonder* (one-dur or one lasting light) of
our lives, that the blood runs deep, and the wound that we suffer from is
in truth a *blessed* sacrament!

---

*Refer back to the discussion of "R" in the main body of the text.